D0707076

How To
Build A Kit Bike

Timothy Remus

Published by:
Wolfgang Publications Inc.
1310 Sunny Slope Lane
Stillwater, MN 55082
http://www.wolfgangpublications.com

First published in 2002 by Wolfgang Publications Inc., 1310 Sunny
Slope Lane, Stillwater MN 55082

ISBN number: 1-929133-11-1

Printed and bound in the USA

How To
Build A Kit Bike

Chapter One

Bike Building 101

Things You Need to Know Before You Start

The idea of building a bike from a pile of parts is both simple and complex, easy and intimidating. On the one hand, what could be simpler. Just connect bracket A to tab B until all the tabs, brackets and bolts equal a complete motorcycle. On the other hand, when you look at all the parts that make up a complete bike, all laid out in one of the "before" pictures, the task of turning all that chaos into a running machine seems overwhelming. Nigh onto impossible.

Dave Perewitz sells a variety of kits, but most popular are his right side drive kits based on a Daytec frame as seen here. You can buy Dave's kits bare or with drivetrain and sheet metal. You can even get Cycle Fab to do part of the assembly.

Yet, thousands of individuals have done exactly that, mostly without the benefit of a kit that contains all or most of the components needed to build the machine.

HISTORY

Very nice motorcycles have been built by men, and sometimes women, for years and years. Long before the advent of the aftermarket, thrifty bikers bought wrecks, scrounged the swap meets for missing or damaged parts and turned the result into a bike for themselves or a machine to sell at a profit.

Many of the first choppers were built from cast-off parts mixed and matched with necessary ape-hanger bars and custom seats. Catalogs like that from Jammer introduced the concept of one-stop-shopping. They would provide everything you needed to build a chopper, from hardtail frame to twenty one inch front rim to peanut tank. There were a few parts missing from those early kits, and you had to provide a complete (or nearly complete) donor bike with engine, transmission, wheel hubs and a variety of hardware items needed to round out the parts missing from the Jammer kit. In those days gone buy there were no complete engines from S&S or TP Engineering; or complete transmissions in four, five or six speeds; or complete primary drive assemblies from Custom Chrome or Biker's Choice.

As we all know, the chopper craze ran its course (the first time) and died an untimely death. The aftermarket industry kind of died at the same time. It wasn't until the mid-1980s that people really started fixing up V-twins again. Arlen Ness introduced us to

The Rocket is a popular soft-tail kit from Custom Chrome. Like the other CCI kits, now called HR3, this kit comes complete with hardware, sheet metal and drivetain, including the 100 cubic inch engine. CCI

Anyone working on a budget might consider this Boulevard kit from Biker's Choice. For about four thousand dollars you get hardtail frame, wheels and tires, sheet metal (fat bob tanks) single seat, bars with controls, and forward controls. Just add engine, drivetrain, wiring and paint. Biker's Choice

Café racers based on the FXR chassis while everyone else was customizing Shovelheads or Softails with wild paint and the first billet parts.

Each year the catalogs offered more parts of better and better quality. Frames, transmission assemblies and complete engines began to fill out the pages in the big books from Drag, Custom Chrome and all the rest. Now you could build a complete bike from scratch, though there were a few parts like rocker boxes and complete wiring harnesses that you had to buy used, from the local Harley-Davidson dealer or make yourself. All the pieces (pun intended) were in place for a resurgence of building bikes from scratch. The catalyst that brought all those pieces together and sent droves of regular riders home to build a bike of their own was the shortage of Harleys that started in the early 1990s.

Quality kits start with a quality frame. Look for frames from well known manufacturers (this example is from Daytec). If you aren't sure about the quality of a frame, ask around at shops that built bikes from scratch, they can tell you what works and what doesn't. Ness

Some people didn't want to wait three years for a new Softail or Dresser. Mechanically inclined riders soon discovered that for the same money as a new factory bike, they could build one from parts. With a trick paint job and a 96 cubic inch engine instead of factory paint and an 80 inch Evo. The entrepreneurs in the group quickly set up small shops to build soft-tails for those without the skills or inclination to build one for themselves. A new industry was born.

For first-time builders, the problem with assembling a complete bike from a catalog is the challenge of matching all the parts. How to know what length tubes will work with a particular frame to provide the

As Cyril Huze explains, "our bike kits never come out of the box with exactly the same components, because we are not only builders, we are also customizers."

desired ride height. Or exactly which set of fenders will provide the look you're after. Some amateur builders learned as they went along, or accepted the fact that it might take three front fenders to get the right one. Lucky builders bought every thing from an experienced shop, a shop they could turn to for occasional help and advice.

THE KIT CONCEPT

It doesn't take the proverbial brain surgeon to see the advantage – for both the seller and buyer - in packaging up more than just a frame. Why not combine *all* the parts into one huge package and sell that? The big companies selling frames and sheet metal soon started to gather parts together in logical groupings. Biker's Choice brought out their Bike in a Box rolling chassis program while Custom Chrome initiated a series of BYOB kits complete with engine, transmission and all the necessary lubricants, nut, bolts and brackets. As Skeeter Todd explains in his interview in Chapter Five. "With one of our kits you know what the silhouette of the bike is going to be." You know before hand which frame and which sheet metal the bike uses and how all those parts look when they're bolted together.

The kit bike concept is growing as we speak. Currently there are at least three of the big catalog companies selling either compete kits or rolling chassis kits. A variety of smaller companies, everyone from Redneck Engineering to Dave Perewitz, are offering kits as complete as you want them. If choosing the engine and drivetrain is something you want to do for yourself, then just buy

Hard to build a bike without a good bench. Air lift benches are available from Handy for less than you might think. Or you can make your own from 2X4s and plywood.

Your custom bike doesn't have to look like everyone else's. Try this rolling soft-tail kit from Cyril Huze. Comes with Cyril's own gas tank and hidden oil tank. Or call for more options. Cyril Huze.

The least expensive soft-tail kit from CCI is this back to basics machine with 130 rear tire, mild ape hanger bars, and all the engine and tranny options offered on the other bikes.

These "Primary in a Box" kits are designed for soft-tail chassis, either early or late, and includes everything but the starter. Biker's Choice

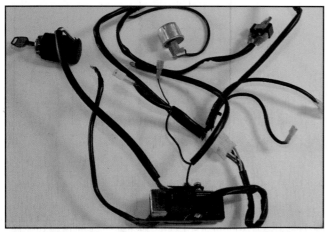

This Wiring Plus kit was used in the Cory Ness project bike. Most kits come in different models depending on ignition switch location and whether or not there are handle-bar switches.

the bare chassis and sheet metal. If you want to make this as easy as possible, then order the chassis kit with a new V-twin, six-speed tranny and belt-drive primary. While the big companies offer a wider variety of kits, from simple hardtails to elaborate soft-tails, the smaller shops often make it easier to add and delete parts to the kits they sell. To upgrade to a bigger motor or different sheet metal.

HOW TO PICK THE RIGHT ONE

Choosing the right motorcycle can be as simple as picking your favorite bike from an article in *Hot Bike* or *American Iron*, or as complex as working through a complete design exercise. Most of us have a bike we've seen in a magazine, at a show or in front of a local hangout that just seems "right." From the paint color to the rake of the fork to the style of seat, this particular bike speaks to us in ways no other bike can. The simplest thing might be to use that perfect machine as the basis of the new bike. If you saw the bike of your dreams in a magazine, then there may be a tech sheet with all the pertinent facts. If it's a local bike, find the owner and strike up a conversation. He or she will likely be flattered that you like the bike enough to ask all the how and why questions.

In spite of the growing number of kits out there, you might not be able to exactly match the dream bike with one of the available kits. Compromise is the nature of life, look at any difference as a chance to break from the mold and make a bike that's more personally yours.

You can also turn the situation around. Instead of trying to make a kit bike match an existing custom machine, why not simply spend time looking at all the available packages and pick the one that strikes your fancy. Make it a point to check out everyone's web site, then stop by the booths at Daytona, Sturgis, Laughlin or one of the other major rally centers. If you've done some research ahead of time it's easier to hone in on the models that most appeal to you, and ask the vendor intelligent questions about that model and any available options.

RACE ROCKET OR TOURING TUB

Though it's all been said before, you need to consider how you will use the new machine. We are in the midst of a Chopper re-birth and if you lust after a Jesse machine or Captain America retro-mobile, that's fine. Most choppers, however, don't make good long-distance mounts. If you want a chopper, or just a custom with a long fork and lots of rake, try to ride a bike with similar geometry so you get a feel for how those particular machines handle.

Among all the different styles of bike available in kit form, the only one missing is a touring rig or dresser (though this may change in the near future). In the past you could by a defacto luxury liner "kit" from Arlen Ness. Based on a rubber-mounted frame, these bikes could be purchased with fairing and bags. With the introduction of the new frame however, (seen a little farther long in this book) Arlen discontinued production of the earlier frame and luxury liner program. Though the situation may change, if you want a kit bike with a fairing you may have to adapt a fairing like the one from Corbin to an existing kit bike.

Deciding how you will really use the bike will have a major impact on the engine you buy as well. It seems nearly everyone you talk to is planning to install a 124 or 126 inch engine in that new bike they're building. A big-inch engine will definitely provide more power than most of us will ever use. As addictive as big power is, you have to consider the cost of that power, both in terms of the outlay of cash and in maintenance.

Tom Pirone, owner of TP Engineering and manufacturer of compete engines, offers a bit of advice. "The motor you choose must match your riding style. Ask the engine manufacturer where the engine makes peak horsepower and torque. If you race you want peak power at high RPM. For me… low end torque is what puts a big smile on my face. There are two kinds of engines. The one that squeezes every possible horse out of the available displacement. And the other that will make good reliable power running on pump gas. Will the engine you're looking at start reliably? Will it need compression

releases? Will it ping? Some engines are so close to the edge that you can't ride them on a hot summer day." For more on engine choices check out Chapter Two, Powertrains.

THINGS YOU NEED

Beyond the kit itself and any missing parts that are not included, the things you need to finish the project include tools, a certain amount of mechanical ability, a willingness to admit you don't know everything (and thus ask someone else for help) and a service manual.

For tools, you need a basic set of end wrenches and sockets, which most readers no doubt already possess. For new comers we've included a chapter on Tools (Chapter Three) that covers both basic hand tools and a few specialized tools you might need. In addition, we've given a brief outline of Tools Needed at the start of each assembly sequence. Remember, many of the specialized tools you might need can be borrowed from a friend or rented.

You do need at least a basic amount of mechanical ability. This is one of those areas where you're going to have to be brutally honest with yourself about mechanical skills or the lack of same. You need to know how tight is tight or at least how to read

Another bike built from a Dave Perewitz/Daytec rolling chassis kit. RSD transmission is from Baker. Rear wheel pulley/brake assembly is from Performance Machine.

11

Nuts and Bolts

What holds your entire motorcycle together is a series of bolts, or bolt and nut combinations. All bolts are graded. Among the best commonly available bolts are grade 8, followed by grade 5 and then grade 3, sometimes called hardware-store grade. Quality bolts are made from forged material and feature rolled threads. Cheap bolts are made from non-forged steel and have threads that are formed by a cutting or smashing. What might be called industrial Allen bolts (Allen is actually a trade name) are nearly always better than a grade 8, it's a standard set by the manufacturers. Chrome Allen bolts are often a grade 5 however, but you won't know unless you ask. Speaking of chrome plated bolts, the chroming process can't get chrome down into the recesses in the head of a bolt and these always rust. The answer is to use those little chrome caps, paint the inside of the hole or put some clear silicone on the end of the Allen wrench the first time you use the bolt.

The other potential problem with chrome bolts is the buildup of material that sometimes occurs. Use a set of taps and dies to chase the threads on any suspect bolts. If in doubt about any bolt, try another. Work through the problem without forcing the bolt into the hole. Anti-seize, or Loctite, on threads will help prevent a busted or stuck bolt because either material will prevent metal-to-metal contact between male and female threads.

Despite their strength and aesthetic appeal, Socket Headed Cap Screws, aka Allen bolts, have a few drawbacks. Like the small head size which means the bolt can't clamp two parts together as effectively as a hex-head bolt unless you use a washer under the head. These bolts are so tough a standard washer will deform under the head of a very tight Allen bolt, so you have to use hardened and ground washers under the head of those SHCS.

Though they look pretty, bolts made from stainless steel (at least the ones we buy in motorcycle and aftermarket shops) aren't very strong. Stainless bolts tend to stretch and distort more than steel as they are tightened. They also tend to gall when screwed onto a stainless nut. For these reasons they should only be used only once with plenty of anti-seize on the threads. Even the stainless bolts rated as grade 8 are suspect because a grade 8 stainless bolt is only equal to about a grade 3 steel bolt.

When looking for bolts to assemble that new V-twin motorcycle consider that some bolts are more important than others. The 1/4 inch bolt that holds the gas tank tab to the frame isn't under nearly the same load as the bolts that locate the caliper to the fork assembly. In the case of the brake caliper, always try to use the bolts that come with the installation kit. For structural, important bolts use the best you can buy. If they don't come with the kit then source them from your local motorcycle shop or a good industrial supply house.

Take the time to read the marking on the head of the bolts and the label on the box. Look for Grade 8 and Made In USA. Avoid anything labeled "better than grade 8," they're usually counterfeit bolts of mediocre quality.

and use a torque wrench. Most kits do not come with a complete set of instructions. Some come with only a packing list. The assembly sequence, specific procedures needed along the way, torque values for all the fasteners, these are all things you need to know or be willing to figure out.

When it comes to figuring things out, a service manual for a bike similar to yours is a great source of information. Inside you will find assembly procedures for many sub-assemblies and torque values for most fasteners used to hold a V-twin motorcycle together. There are even some diagnostic charts for those occasions when the finished bike or sub-assembly doesn't work (oops).

The other priceless source of information is the shop where you bought the kit and any extra parts. Consider buying everything from a local shop with a good reputation for customer service. When it comes time to assemble the inner primary or figure out whether or not to use Loctite on a particular bolt, there's no one with better information than the counter people and mechanics from a good shop. It's possible you will need help with things like the wiring or alignment of the drivetrain — occasions where it's nice to have a good relationship with the shop down the street.

WHAT'S IT ALL GOING TO COST?

The cost of a kit bike runs from somewhere around 12,000.00 to well over 20,000.00. On the low end there's the very basic soft-tail or hardtail kit from Custom Chrome. As Michael Marquart, a sales rep for Custom Chrome explains, "The cheapest kit is the Nemesis soft-tail, a 180 rear-tire soft-tail, retail is almost thirteen thousand dollars. But the street price is much lower than that because dealers are doing a lot of discounting. I tell people to add about six hundred to a thousand dollars for a nice paint job, that's from the local body shop. A nice paint job with a molded frame starts at fifteen hundred dollars."

"I discourage people from buying a frame and then a motor and then all the rest," explains Mike. "CCI gives you a discount to buy the package, at least two thousand dollars, and you don't worry about what fits what."

If that's still too much, you could always buy the least expensive hardtail rolling chassis kit you can find, and combine that with a used 80 inch Evo and used five speed transmission. To quote Mike Marquart again, "What I call take-out Evos are about two thousand dollars, and I still see new satin-finish Evos discounted by the dealers that sell for about twenty seven hundred dollars but that's with no carb and no ignition. The cheapest RevTech motor, the 88 inch motor, sells for four thousand dollars. It's silver too but it comes with carb and ignition and chrome covers and tappet blocks. A used five-speed transmission is eight hundred to a thousand dollars, and new ones from the catalog are only about twelve hundred dollars."

"You have to allow extra for polishing and chrome, or fabrication work. If a guy doesn't have the tools, like I don't have the impact wrench you need and the 1-1/4 inch socket for the compensator sprocket. Bleeding the brakes is not always the easiest thing, that's not an easy thing to do by yourself, but all those jobs are easily done by most shops and it usually doesn't cost that much."

TAKE YOUR TIME, GET IT DONE RIGHT

No matter which kit you decide to buy or modify, you have to remember just a few pertinent facts. First, you will probably farm some of the work out, and that's OK. Second, unless you've built a couple of bikes before, there will be things you don't know, and that's OK too as long as you're willing to admit it. Third, haste does make waste, and even at the bottom of the price range, there's too much money at stake here to start throwing it away. Forth, it's good to be creative but if no one else has ever done it that way, there's probably a good reason. Finally, you have to keep plugging away. Even in professional shops with more than one person working on the bike it takes three to five days to assemble a simple kit. That does not include paint or running for parts or stopping to scratch your head. Plan for the long term, don't assume it will only take a week. Instead, be sure you get something done every week so the project doesn't stall in the corner of the garage for six months in a half-finished condition.

Biker's Choice kits come without the hand grips or brakes, so you can pick the most personal parts of the bike yourself. Biker's Choice

Chapter Two

Drivetrain

Engines, Trannys & Primary Drives

While some of the kits mentioned in this book come complete with engine, transmission and primary, others are really only rolling chassis kits that require the builder to choose and buy the powertrain. For that reason we've included an abbreviated list of engine options, transmission choices and primary considerations. When in doubt as to which combination of engine, transmission and primary will work best with a particular kit, it's good to ask the advice of the manufacturer.

If choosing the engine, transmission, inner and outer primary, starter and all the hardware sounds like too many decisions to make, take the easy way out with this DriveTrain kit. Options include plain, polished or black/chrome finish, 88, 100 or 110 inch engine, and early or late soft-tail inner and outer primary. CCI

Complete Twin Cam and Evo engines are available from your local dealer in at least two finish levels. TC engines come in three displacements: 88, 95 and 103 cubic inches

POWER, POWER, POWER

No matter which style of bike you buy it will have a V-twin heart. Most kits come with, or are designed for, an Evo-style drivetrain. However, more and more frames and thus kits, are being offered with mounts that will accept the TC 88B. A short discussion of frames and engines is appropriate at this point. Up until the year 2000 models, all factory Softails used an Evo engine bolted directly into the frame. Dyna and Dresser models by contrast used, and still use, a rubber-mounted engine to quell the vibrations of a typical V-twin engine. Starting in 2000, factory Softails came with a TC 88B engine equipped with counter balancers. The counter balancers eliminate all but the worst of the vibration and essentially eliminate the need for rubber mounts.

What all this means is that pre-2000 style softtail frames (identified by the welded-in center post) are generally designed to accept an Evo-style engine, either from the factory or the aftermarket. A non-B style of TC 88 engine can usually be adapted into one of these frames with the help of an adapter plate at the back of the motor that takes the place of the

rear motor mount boss on an Evo. The TC 88B engine mounts in a completely different manner and must be installed in a frame designed for the B engine, and must also be mated to the factory transmission (for more on the use of the B engine in a kit bike see the Biker's Choice assembly sequence).

Evo and non-B engines bolted directly to the frame cause the whole bike to vibrate. The degree to which the bike shakes and whether or not it's a good thing will depend on the size of the engine, the brand of frame, the gearing and personal opinion. If the new machine is intended for short trips the

S&S offers their bullet-proof engines in displacements up to 124 cubic inches, with bigger motors on the way. Can be ordered assembled or in pieces with moderate or high compression.

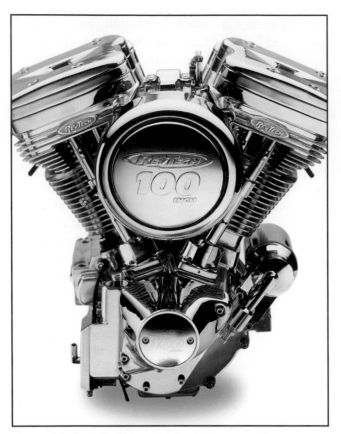

Assembled in their own ISO 9000 manufacturing plant, the RevTech engines come complete in 88, 100 and 110 cubic inch displacements. Order yours polished or in raw aluminum.

vibration probably isn't a consideration – you simply need to understand the difference. The only way to guarantee a vibration free ride is to use a B motor or a rubber-mounted engine and transmission like the one installed in the Y2K Cory Ness sequence.

ENGINE OPTIONS

Twin Cam

For all those riders who want the latest engine from Milwaukee, complete TC 88 engines are available from your local dealer. George from Delano Harley-Davidson reports that both A and B Twin Cam motors are available complete at prices that start at $3495.00 for an A motor in silver and polish. A TC 88B in black and chrome is $4995.00. The B motor is available with the 95 inch kit already installed for $5995.00 in silver and chrome but it comes set up for fuel injection, with manifold and injectors. A better bet would be to buy a 88 inch engine and then the piston kit from H-D (which comes in various compression ratios). Complete transmissions are available as well, starting at $1395.00 for an Evo-style Softail.

There is no shortage of parts from both Screamin' Eagle and the aftermarket to make the newer TC motor howl. For an increase in displacement there are the well known 95 inch kits from SE (you can now buy complete motors with the 95 inch kit already installed), and similar big-bore kits from the aftermarket. Additional increases in displacement can be had through the installation of a stroker kit. By increasing the stock 3-3/4 inch bore to 4 inches, and the stock 4 inch stroke to 4-5/8 inches, the displacement can be boosted to 116 cubic inches with kits from companies like Jim's, S&S or Zipper's. There are also hop up kits from Head Quarters and others that retain the stock displacement, boosting power through the use of ported heads and new camshafts. There's even a factory stroker kit that bumps the displacement to 103 cubes.

Evo

The Evo engine is available in about a thousand different configurations. Everything from 80 inch

Brand new Shovelheads are available, complete with carburetor in sizes that start at 80 and top out at 103 cubic inches. S&S

factory engines to Mondo 124 cubic inch torquesters from TP Engineering, S&S, Kendall Johnson and others. In case those aren't big enough, even bigger mills are just around the corner. A discussion of the Evo must include the original 80 inch example from Milwaukee. With everyone focused on the big block examples from the aftermarket, it's easy to forget that the original Evo is a great engine. By adding more cam and compression these engines put out an easy 80 horsepower and 80 foot pounds of torque. Plenty of power with the majority of it available relatively low in the RPM range where most of us ride.

Harley-Davidson dealers can still order new Evo engines from the factory. To quote George again, "silver and polished Evos retail for $2995.00 and the factory says there is no plan to discontinue those engines." These engines come with warranty but ship without carb or alternator. Street prices may vary.

Because a number of riders are replacing 80 inch Evos with much bigger aftermarket engines there are some really good deals to be had on complete used Evos. Before snapping up that great deal, remember that the motor isn't any good unless it's legal. The laws vary state by state (see Title Considerations in Chapter Eight), but it's not a good idea to buy any engine unless you have a legal MSO that will satisfy the authorities in your state.

Early Engine Options

Though most riders will install either an Evo or TC engine, there are complete early-style motors and parts readily available. S&S offers complete Shovelhead engines with either alternator or generator cases. You can even buy a hybrid that offers the look of a generator case yet uses an alternator to produce the juice. Add a pair of Panheads to the Shovel and you've got yourself a new Panhead. Or buy a complete Pan-Demonium Pan from CSI. Accurate Engineering is a company that assembles complete early style engines, from Knuckles to

Shovels in various displacements and either early or late cases. Knucklehead Power is another purveyor of complete Knuckles, or complete bikes powered by a new Knuckle.

Because the engine mounting pads are the same on a Shovelhead as they are on an Evo-style V-twin, a shovel or Panhead will drop into the Evo frame. Evos are generally taller than the earlier engines so height isn't an issue when using an older-style engine in a frame meant for an Evo.

Most of these re-born engine designs have been modified to work with modern primary drives – but you don't know that unless you ask. Though we offer some primary guidance farther along, with older engines it's often beneficial to work with an experienced counter person or aftermarket company like BDL or Primo/Rivera who can match up the engine, transmission, primary drive and starter.

Known as an innovator, TP Engineering sells engines that are durable, powerful and very easy on the eyes. Available fully polished with their own rocker covers.

Biker's Choice sells complete, and nearly complete engines from TP Engineering (shown) and S&S to round out their rolling chassis kits. You can follow the engine manufacturer's recommendation as to cam and valve gear or try to come up with a better combination on your own. Biker's Choice

TRANSMISSIONS

Most builders are going to use a five or six-speed transmission. Use of a four-speed transmission will require a frame designed to accommodate the early transmission.

Kits designed for an Evo engine are typically designed to accept a late-model five-speed transmission. Five-speed transmissions are now manufactured and assembled by a large number of companies. Soft-tail and hardtail frames nearly always take the typical "soft-tail" transmission, i.e. a transmission case that is designed to mount to the frame without being bolted to the back of the engine in any way.

Among the companies that manufacture and sell complete transmissions is the big motorcycle company in Milwaukee. Complete transmissions, or just bare cases, are available from any Harley-Davidson dealer. Harley-Davidson made a major change in their transmissions in about 1994 when they began

the conversion to high contact gears. Ground in such a way as to reduce noise and increase strength, these gears can't be mixed with other non HCR gears.

Softail-style five-speed cases are nearly the same from 1986 to 1999. However, factory transmissions built prior to 1990 used a tapered mainshaft, which required the appropriate clutch basket. Transmissions built after 1990 used a straight mainshaft, and use a much stronger clutch assembly. Thus the most common complete five-speed transmissions are often listed as 1990 – 1999.

Six-speeds

Baker Transmission was the first to introduce a six-speed transmission in 1998. Today there are at least two other firms making six-speed transmissions. The beauty of these transmissions with the extra gear is the fact that the case is the same as a five-speed case, and the mainshaft is the same as a five-speed mainshaft. So a primary assembly that works with a late-model five-speed will work just as well with a

The Panhead you buy doesn't have to come from a swap meet. This example is brand new, from the generator cases to the cast iron cylinders and aluminum heads - in displacements up to 103 cubic inches. Accurate Engineering

new six-speed. For the same reason, six-speed gearsets will fit into a standard five-speed case.

The Baker transmission is available with either a .86 or .80 to 1 overdrive ratio, which will drop the RPM at 70 mph by 475 and 680 RPM respectively. The RevTech six-speed transmission comes with a sixth gear ratio of .893 to one.

SPEEDOMETERS.

Late model Harley-Davidsons use electronic speedometers, connected to a pickup in the transmission. Obviously you have to decide during the early part of the planning process whether your speedometer will be electronic or mechanical. Nearly all new complete five and six-speed transmissions have the correct gears and the small port in the case designed to accept the sensor. The factory began the switch to electronic speedometers in 1994, so transmissions listed in the catalog as "1991 to 1994 Softail" might not be equipped to drive an electronic speedometer.

All the Baker six-speed transmissions are equipped to drive an electronic speedometer, and probably other brands as well. For anyone who wants to run a mechanical speedometer there are two basic styles and two current ratios. Two-to-one speedometers were used mostly with FX and FXR bikes equipped with nineteen inch front wheels and narrow glide forks. A second ratio, 2240:1, was used with Softails with twenty one inch front wheels and wide glide forks.

You have to match the front end, forks and the wheel diameter to the right style of drive unit. Then match that drive unit to a speedometer with a matching ratio. And you still need the right cable in the right length with the correct fittings on either end, though this isn't as hard as it might sound.

HOW TO CONNECT ENGINE AND TRANSMISSION

Choosing the correct inner and outer primary housing, along with matching starter and hardware, can be confusing. If the bike uses an Evo and five-speed transmission, then you have the option of running the standard chain-style primary with all the matching components.

Even a simple application like a late-model Evo and five-speed, however, still requires you to get the right inner and outer primary covers, with the finish you need, designed for forward controls, along with the compensator sprocket, the chain itself, matching clutch assembly and matching starter motor. A number of companies make it easier to buy the correct primary assembly – they've assembled kits that include matching components for late-model applications.

Among these kits is a complete primary assembly, without a starter, from Biker's Choice for 1989 to 1993 Softails and another for 1994 – 2000 Softails. Custom Chrome offers very similar kits, with or without heavy duty Kevlar clutch. All factory bikes from 1994 on use the same gear-reduction

Here you can see the extended mainshaft gearset compared to a standard gearset. This is one more way to get the belt or chain over to the left far enough that it will clear the tire.

Twin Cam "B" engines (shown) must use the correct and matching transmission case from Harley-Davidson. "A" engines can bolt up to a standard five-speed case with the use of an adapter.

starter, so by using the 1994 and later inner and outer primary you can also use the late model starter.

When using Shovel or Panhead engines there are no primary kits. You have to find the right inner primary to connect the engine and transmission. The clutch hub must fit the transmission mainshaft. New Shovelheads can likely be matched up with five-speed transmissions through the use of a 1970 and up inner primary, but you may want to purchase all the parts from one shop to ensure everything fits together.

Belt Primary

Belts come in a variety of widths, some narrow enough to fit inside a conventional inner and outer primary housing, some so wide there aren't any housings big enough to house them. BDL, Primo and Karata all offer primary drive assemblies that include engine sprocket, belt and clutch assembly, designed to replace a conventional chain primary. Finding the right belt for your application can be accomplished by spending time at one of the web sites or with a catalog. Belts are also a good way to connect unusual combinations of components, like a pre-Evo engine with a four or five-speed transmission.

Offset drivetrains and RSD

The only realistic way to run right side drive (RSD) is with a frame designed from the start for RSD. But before we begin a brief discussion of RSD, it's necessary to back up and explain the evolution that led up to RSD. Just to clarify, in the examples that follow we are talking about typical pre-2000 soft-tail drivetrains, i.e. engine and transmission bolted into the frame as separate components.

Transmission cases come in a wide range of shapes. Most Evo-powered hard and soft-tails will use a "soft-tail" style of transmission case.

To create clearance between ever-larger rear tires and the final drive belt it is necessary to move the tire/wheel to the right or the belt to the left. Most frames that accept 200 and wider rear tires make room for the belt by offsetting the transmission, and sometimes the engine, to the left.

Because the engine and transmission are separate units, it's relatively easy to offset the transmission to the left while leaving the engine in the center, or close to center, of the frame.

Early Wide Tire Kits were nothing more than a spacer used between the left side of the engine and the inside of the inner primary, an offset transmission mounting plate, and a spacer for the compensating sprocket. Those early kits moved the transmission over a maximum of 1/2 inch. New kits and frame designs position the transmission as much as an inch to the left.

Most current frames meant for 230 and 250 section rear tires utilize a wider rear frame section as well as an offset transmission. However, at some point the offset weight will affect the balance of the bike. This is not static weight either, but spinning weight with it's own gyroscopic effect.

Right side drive

The solution to ever-expanding offsets is a right hand drive transmission. Baker Drivetrain is offering for sale both five and six-speed transmissions with right hand drive. RSD allows frame designers to put the engine in the center with only a small amount of transmission offset, for a bike with good basic balance.

This new transmission uses many standard five-speed parts, and a standard five-speed case, though the shift drum and forks, main and counter shafts and fifth (and sixth) gear are specific to the new right-side transmission. Like their standard five and six-speed transmission, the gears inside this new RSD transmission are manufactured by Andrews. As we stated before, the chassis used must be designed from the start to run right side drive.

Complete six-speed transmissions are available for Twin Cam B applications. Custom Chrome

Soft-tail style transmission assemblies are available complete, in five- or six-speed configurations. Biker's Choice

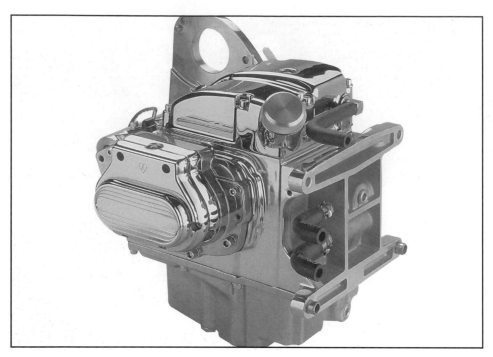

Designed for the TC 88A, this complete transmission assembly is available with a polished case, with or without an extended mainshaft already installed. Arlen Ness

Extended mainshafts

The Cory Ness Y2K bike in Chapter Six utilizes a Dyna drivetrain, the engine and transmission are bolted together into one unit. Moving the belt over far enough to clear the 250 rear tire is done by installing a transmission with a longer mainshaft. The same trick can be used on bikes with TC 88 engine and transmission, which are likewise bolted together into one assembly.

Belt or Chain?

The toothed belt final drive we all take for granted offers the efficiency of a chain without the mess or maintenance. Prior to the introduction of the 2000 models the factory Big Twins used a 1-1/2 inch belt while Sportsters used a 1-1/8 inch belt. The larger belt worked well and needed little maintenance, even when abused by heavy riders with a knack for leaving their calling card on the pavement.

The use of big aftermarket engines with 124 and more cubes has altered that picture somewhat. Belt drive can still be used with big engines, it all depends on the rider. A heavy rider or one who rides hard will soon have a string of trophies (broken belts) hanging from nails in the garage. Ultimately it depends on the size of the engine, how you use that power and the weight of bike and rider. Some of the kits (CCI for example) run a 1-1/8 inch final drive belt, as a way of obtaining a bit more clearance for the phat rear tire. These narrower belts are said to be reinforced, and just as strong as the wider belts used for so long on Big Twins. There are a few final drive

More and more people are running a number 530 chain instead of a belt for final drive. These O-ring, nickel plated chains come in six lengths, from 102 to 120 links. CCI

belts even narrower than 1-1/8 inch but there should be considered "for show use only."

Heavy Metal

Chain final drive is showing up on more and more aftermarket bikes and kits, like the soft-tail chopper from American Thunder seen farther along in this book. A chain leaves more room for fat tires and makes it easy to change final drive ratios. Best of all, unless the bike has a ten inch slick out back, you aren't going to break a chain.

Nearly all final drive chains are a number 530, though even within that designation there are heavy duty, O-ring and nickel plated chains to suit every rider. Sprockets for both the transmission and the rear wheel are available in various sizes from all the major catalogs as well as Baker and Andrews.

THE FINAL WORD

Those of you buying complete kits will have it easy. Engine, transmission and primary drive are all there. No offsets to worry about or questions about chain drive. The rest will have to sort through the large number of options. Frame design will determine the major components, though you are still left to ponder the primary and the best type of final drive.

Don't be afraid to ask questions from the frame manufacturer or the shop where you buy the kit. Consider how the bike will be used before deciding to buy the latest 4 inch external belt drive from Rivera. If it's a relatively mild engine and you aren't prone to public displays of power, then a standard chain primary and belt drive will be more than adequate.

Buy your parts from known entities. Kits, like primary kits, often save time, hassle and money. Though it sounds obvious, buy parts that will work together.

This 3 inch belt drive can be ordered for the latest soft-tails, TC 88B applications, and early Shovelheads. Comes complete with motorplate, that takes the place of a conventional inner primary, and the belt guard. Rivera/Primo

The Brute II system utilizes an 11mm belt and heavy duty Pro-clutch in one package designed for most pre-Evo engine applications. Rivera/Primo

Chapter Three

Tools 'r Cool

Gleaming Jewelry

The best mechanic in the world can't fix a thing without some tools. Tools are, by their nature, an integral and essential part of this building process. Tools are more than that however. There's something about the feel of a nice combination wrench as it sits in your hand, or the look of a set of tools laid out neatly on the bench. A set of tools has an intrinsic power, a potential. They represent your ability to be creative, self-sufficient and productive.

Judging by the calls the tech-line people at

Though you may not need all the tools seen here, a set of tools is one of the best investments you can make. Long after the current project is finished, the tools will still be there - necessary components if you want the satisfaction of doing it yourself.

Custom Chrome and Arlen Ness receive, there are some neophyte mechanics putting bike kits together. So if you already own a huge roll-away tool box filled with all the goodies from Snap-on or Craftsman, skip this chapter. For the rest of our readers we've laid out the basic tools needed to assemble a complete bike, and a few of the special tools needed along the way as well. Don't think of it as additional money you're spending to build the bike. Think of it as an investment – good tools truly do last a lifetime.

QUALITY AND COST

The name we've all come to accept as synonymous with quality tools is Snap-on. Most of these tools are so beautiful is seems a shame to put 'em on a greasy bolt or nut. Break one and the tool man will give you another. When it comes to tools, these are about as good as it gets. That doesn't mean you have to take a third mortgage on the house (assuming the second mortgage was taken out to buy the bike kit) to purchase a ten thousand dollar set of gleaming Snap-on tools, all housed in a roll-away that's so big it needs it's own small motor so you can roll it around the garage.

There is nothing wrong with buying Craftsman or S-K or some other quality brand of tool, for a lot less than Snap-on prices. In fact, there are some good reasons to patronize the local Sears outlet or auto parts store. Beyond price, the advantages include the ability to quickly get a replacement tool when you do break the occasional socket – without having to go looking for one of those big white and red trucks.

The Snap-on driver will often tout the advantages of

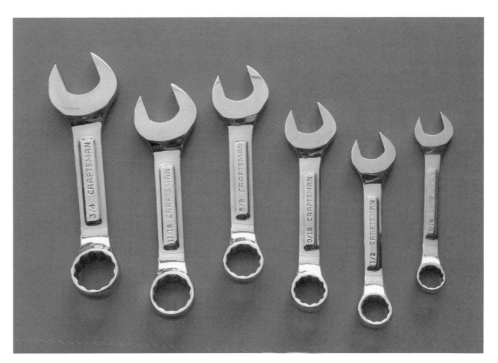

Perhaps the handiest wrench ever invented, a combination wrench combines the speed and convenience of an open-end wrench with the gripping ability of a box-end. Available either short, for getting into tight spaces, or longer for more leverage.

Sockets come in every flavor from vanilla to chocolate chip. On the bottom are the 3/8 inch deep "impact" sockets (impact meaning they're strong enough to be used with an impact wrench). On top are conventional 1/2 inch sockets.

Snap-on tools. The fact that the sockets and box-end wrenches do grab the nut just right so the wrench is less likely to slip or strip the head. And how the socket extensions are thicker in cross section than some of those other brands and thus absorb less torque when you're really reefing on a bolt. Yet, most of us are only weekend, shade-tree mechanics. Whether we really need the extra quality is open to debate.

There's an undeniable prestige factor that comes with the Snap-on logo. That fact alone should not be the determining factor. Buy quality tools that are guaranteed against breakage. The actual brand you use and the amount you spend will depend on how deep your pockets are and how much you really expect to use the tools.

METRIC AND AMERICAN TOOLS

Despite the metrification of the world around us, American V-twins are still assembled almost exclusively from fasteners measured in inches instead of millimeters. The biggest exception is the nut and bolt used to connect the battery cables to the terminals. Because the batteries come from overseas most of these fasteners are 10 mm. This just happens to be one of those metric sizes that doesn't cross over to an American size. 10mm is too small to use a 7/16 inch wrench and too big for a 3/8 inch. So you either need a 10mm combination wrench in your set - or a small vise grip.

A BASIC SET OF TOOLS

Socket wrenches

Socket wrenches are categorized by the size of the square drive on the ratchet. Most mechanics own 1/4, 3/8 and 1/2 inch socket sets. If you can only own one, the sockets that come with a 3/8 inch set will fit ninety percent of the nuts on a motorcycle and many cars.

Deep sockets are exactly that, deeper so they will drop over a nut that's screwed onto a bolt that's a little too long and leaves an inch of threads extending past the nut. Sockets come in six and twelve-point styles, with twelve point the default setting with most sets. As always, for everything you gain you likewise give something up. Six-point sockets are stronger and less likely to slip off a nut that's really tight or already rounded off. But the thicker walls mean that a six-point socket won't fit over a nut or bolt that's set into a really tight spot.

Most 1/2 inch sets only go to 1-1/8th inch, which might be just fine except that the big fastener that holds the compensator sprocket on most of these machines measures 1-1/4, or more, inches.

Combination wrenches

One of the handiest wrenches ever invented, a combination wrench is one that combines an open-end wrench on one end with a box-wrench at the other. For fittings and fasteners that aren't very tight, the open-end wrench is ideal. The box end of the combination wrench gets a much better grip on the nut or bolt head and is definitely the one to use to loosen or tighten a nut. You can even combine two combination wrenches (one becomes the cheater-bar for the other) for additional leverage. The most common sets of combination wrenches start at 3/8 inch and go to 3/4 inch. Like the

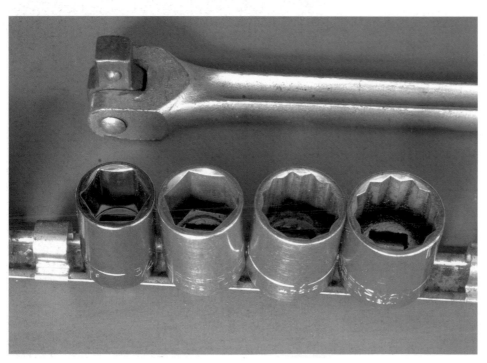

Six-point sockets like those on the left are less likely to slip on a nut or bolt, but are also a little thicker and harder to get into really right spaces.

3/8 inch socket sets, this range will fit most fasteners most of the time. Exceptions include many axle nuts and, possibly, the pivot bolt on some soft-tail chassis.

Allen wrenches

As mentioned elsewhere, Allen is actually a trade name (thus the capital letter). What we call Allen bolts are actually socket headed cap screws (SHCS). None the less, the wrenches used to turn a SHCS are still referred to as Allen wrenches.

For anyone who plans to assemble or work on V-twin bikes, a good set of Allen wrenches is essential. The specialized tools come in a couple of varieties. Most commonly found on the tool board are the simple sets that start at 1/8 inch or less and go to 3/8 inch. For starters you might want to buy a deluxe kit, one that includes sizes both smaller and larger than those mentioned just above. There are also some seldom-used sizes that are handy to have and that only come with the more complete sets.

Allen wrenches come in a variety of styles, from straight to ball-end. Ball end Allen wrenches are kind of like a universal socket without the universal joint. Given the number of Allen bolts on most V-twins ball-end Allens are nearly a must-have item. You can buy either straight Allen or the ball-end variety attached to a socket-end which makes them easy to use with a ratchet or even an impact wrench.

MORE SPECIALIZED TOOLS

Tap and Die sets

Among the non-essential but extremely handy tools you might purchase is a tap and die set. Though most of us think of a tap or die as something used to cut threads, most are actually used to clean and repair existing threads. The best threads are rolled and not cut. Though you can cut threads for a bolt with a light load or in an emergency, the tap and die set is used mostly to clean all the threads taped in the frame, to clean excess chrome from some plated nuts or bolts (for easier assembly) and to chase the threads in a situation where you just can't get the nut or bolt started. If there's extra money in the tool budget, spend it here. We should mention that Snap-on and some others make taps and dies meant specifically for chasing threads.

Torque Wrenches

How tight is tight? The accurate answer can only be answered with a torque wrench. There is a torque specification for most of the bolts used to assemble a

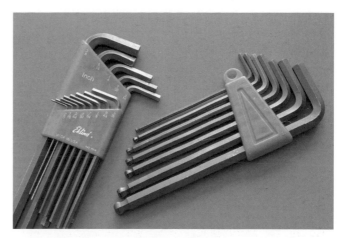

If you're going to work on V-twin powered motorcycles, you need at least one, probably two, sets of Allen wrenches.

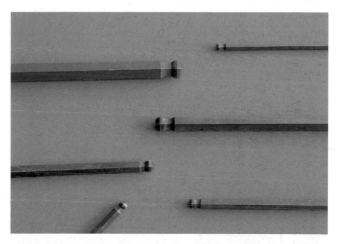

Known as ball-end Allens, the rounded end works like a universal joint without the joint.

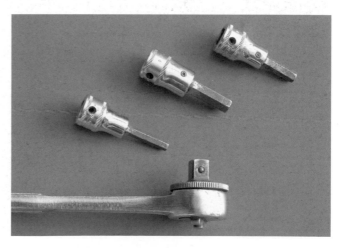

Allen wrenches, both regular and ball-end, are available in 3/8 inch drive models for attachment to your ratchet or air tools.

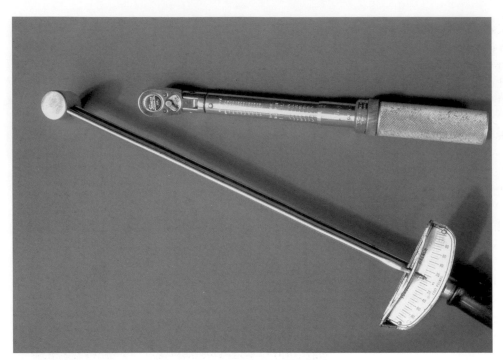

Whether you use an old pointer-style torque wrench like that on the bottom or the more common "clicker" style, torque readings must be taken while the wrench is in motion.

V-twin powered motorcycle. Beginners and experienced hands alike would do well to follow these torque recommendations, especially for critical engine and chassis bolts.

It takes more torque to start a bolt moving than it does to keep it moving. Torque readings must be made with the wrench in motion. The wrenches themselves come in at least three varieties.

Least expensive of the various torque wrench designs is the deflecting beam. Looking like a breaker bar with a pointer and gauge attached, this tried and true design is simple, effective and inexpensive. Just put the socket on the end and put a nice steady pull on the handle until the needle lines up with the desired reading on the foot-pound scale. The trouble with this very basic torque wrench is the relatively large size and lack of any pivoting head, meaning it can be hard to get into tight spots. You must also be able to see the foot pound scale while putting torque on the nut or bolt.

A more high-tech solution to the problem of precisely tightening those SHCS holding the rotor to the hub is provided by the "clicker" type of torque wrench. Like a cricket, these wrenches click, but only when you've hit the desired torque. A micrometer style handle allows you to set the torque, typically in one-pound increments.

Clicker-style torque wrenches are very popular and for good reason. First, they include a ratchet head, so in essence the torque

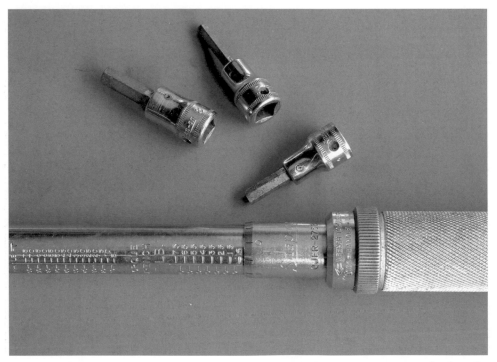

Clicker style torque wrenches have a micrometer-style gauge, just turn the handle to the desired setting and pull until it "clicks." Be sure to store the wrench with the handle at its lowest setting.

wrench becomes a big ratchet. Second, most have a flex-head, meaning it's easier to get them into tight spots. Third, they do not require that you be able to see the scale while turning the bolt. Additionally, they are generally smaller than a deflecting-beam style of torque wrench.

Clicker style torque wrenches are by far the most common, despite their higher cost (as compared to deflector-beam torque wrenches) and the fact that the wrench should be set to its lowest setting after every use.

What might be called the dial-style torque wrench rounds out our selection. These are similar to a deflector-beam but instead of a pointer and scale, the wrench has a round dial that indicates the torque. The more expensive models have a light and tone that indicates you've hit the torque setting so you don't have to look right at the dial as you turn the torque wrench.

Though quite accurate these torque wrenches suffer from many of the same ills that trouble the deflector-beam designs. Namely, they are physically big and have no ratchet head, making them hard to use especially in confined spaces.

WIRING WORK

Some builders are going to farm-out the wiring work, but for those who decide to tackle the job themselves there are a few necessary tools.

For crimping the small wire ends onto the individual wires before you stick them in the terminal blocks (see the assembly in Chapter Four) you need a very high quality crimping tool. A tool that crimps the terminal onto both the bare wire end and the insulation. If you use anything else the wire end won't slide neatly into the plastic block, or the little tang that holds the wire end into the terminal block will be damaged so the wire end slips back out of the block later causing weird and hard

to diagnose electrical maladies. The good ones are called G.M. style crimping tools and can be purchased from a good tool truck or tool outlet.

The other necessary tool is a soldering iron. Buy a gun-style iron with at least 150 watts of power and practice on some scrap wire if you've never used one before.

BUY THE GOOD STUFF

The tools we've outlined are only a beginning. We haven't talked about air tools or compressors for example. But how bad do you really need a compressor? Yes, they're nice, but you don't have to build this by the clock, so are air tools really needed? When it comes time to tighten the compensator sprocket (this large fastener is often tightened with a large socket on a 1/2 inch impact wrench) take the bike down to the local bike shop.

How many tools you buy and how much they cost is up to you. You don't have to spend the most for the best. Conversely, don't take the opposite approach and try to spend the very least for the worst, or cheapest el-gypo stuff out there.

You don't have to sell the second car to pay for a set of tools. Basic tool sets, available from Sears and other hardware outlets, offer a surprisingly good value for anyone undertaking their first big project.

Chapter Four

RevTech Soft-Tail

The Goliath Runs

Custom Chrome was one of the first to offer a complete bike kit with their BYOB (Build Your Own Bike) program started just a few years ago. The assembly of the Goliath kit, documented here, is one of the more radical kits offered by

CCI (Custom Chrome Incorporated) and comes with the mandatory 250X18 Avon rear tire, 21 inch front tire and stretched Santee soft-tail frame.

Note: While the assembly of this kit can be used as a guide for the assembly of most soft-tail

The finished project, a very hot soft-tail built from the Goliath kit, complete with a completely polished 100 cubic inch V-twin engine and six-speed transmission. CCI's BYOB program is now known as "HR3."

TOOLS YOU NEED

The tools needed to assemble this bike include the following: A complete set of "Allen" wrenches (Allen is actually a trade name), a set of combination wrenches up to about 1 inch, a set of socket wrenches in 1/4, 3/8 and 1/2 inch drives. You will also need a tap and die set, a good "GM" style crimping tool, a soldering iron and a heat gun (or small cigarette lighter) to heat the shrink wrap. A compressor and half inch impact

Out of the box (think of a refrigerator crate) the kit looks like this. Kendall went ahead and had the frame and swingarm powder coated right away.

type bikes, there are specific instructions and specifications seen here that apply only to these particular Custom Chrome kits.

Note number two: While this kits and others are sold on the premise that you can Build Your Own Bike, some parts of the assembly are much easier if you've done them before. What we're trying to say is that you might want to ask for help with a couple of things, like the wiring and preparation of the inner primary. Don't be afraid to ask for help, or possibly take the bike to the shop where you bought the kit for help with difficult parts of the assembly.

The assembly shown here took place in the shop of Kendall Johnson in Germanton, North Carolina. Custom Chrome has enough confidence in their frames that they recommend sending the frame out for painting or powder coating right away – without doing a full mock up. And Kendall did exactly that. So the first pictures show the unpacked kit with a painted frame. We should mention the fact that CCI does recommend mocking up the sheet metal, to make sure it fits the bike and that all the mounting holes line up, before having it painted.

The engine that came with this kit is the fully polished (optional) 100 cubic inch RevTech mill, with Mikuni carburetor and ignition.

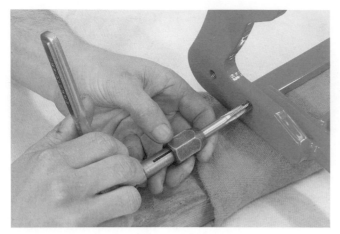

Before assembly can begin all the tapped holes must be cleaned so there is no powder on the threads.

Then the engine is set into the frame for the same reason. If you have more time this can be done before the powder paint is applied.

By using a known "system" Kendall was able to match the powder paint to the liquid paint used on the sheet metal.

Here you can see where the outline of the engine was marked off.

The transmission mounting plate must be set in place and marked so the area underneath can be ground clean.

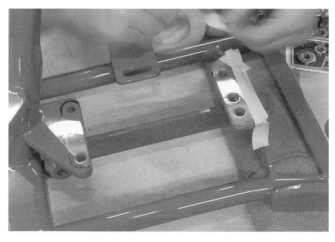

Next the area to be ground clean must be masked off.

wrench is handy but hardly essential. There are a few special tools needed as well, (you might be able to rent or borrow these) including the driver you need for installation of the races for the neck bearings, and drivers or adapters needed for installation of the bushings that must be pressed into the inner and outer primary housing. All the fasteners used in this kit are measured in inches. There are no metric fasteners and no need for metric wrenches or sockets.

PREPARATION

After having the frame powder coated all the tapped holes are cleaned out with the appropriate tap. It's also a good idea to compare the parts in your kit with the packing list, and inspect the parts themselves to make sure none were damaged during shipping.

After setting the frame up on a bench the RevTech engine is uncrated. This kit came with the 100 cubic inch engine. As an option, the engine was ordered already polished. Their engines are test run prior to shipping and each one comes with a colored chart that shows the RPM, temperature and oil pressure recorded during the short test run.

The engine and transmission must mount onto bare steel, not a painted surface. This makes for a better electrical ground and avoids the possibility that paint between the engine and frame will become pulverized later and leave you with loose bolts. Because the frame was sent out for painting before those areas could be masked off, the engine and transmission mounting points must now be marked and the paint ground off.

Bolts are included in the kit and they came two ways. Some are kits, packaged for a particular job, like "engine mounting bolts," while others are simply sent in small plastic bags. Kendall and the boys laid out all the bolts that weren't packaged into kits, on a piece of cardboard, and sorted them into logical groupings.

ASSEMBLY BEGINS

Once the engine and transmission mounting areas are free of paint, and the correct bolts are identified, the engine can be set into the frame with the bolts snug, and the transmission plate can

A small air-powered grinder is used to clean the powder paint off the areas where the motor will sit on the frame.

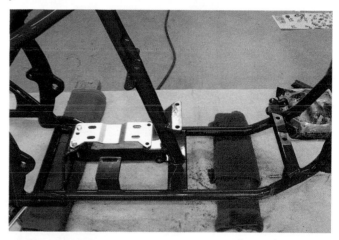

After carefully grinding off the paint the engine-transmission mounting areas look like this.

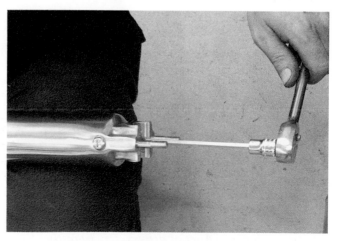

A bolt with sealing washer under its head comes up from the bottom of each lower leg, as shown, to hold the fork together.

The kit comes with fork oil of the correct viscosity, which must be carefully measured before being poured into the fork tube.

The regency triple trees must be partially assembled before they can be put on the bike.

You may have to clean the paint or powder out of the neck before the races are installed.

Installing the races is done with a driver as shown. "A set of drivers can be picked up at any good tool house," explains Kendall, "or a good auto parts store."

The triple tree assembly comes up from the bottom.

Like the engine, the area under the regulator must be clean of paint so the regulator has a good ground circuit.

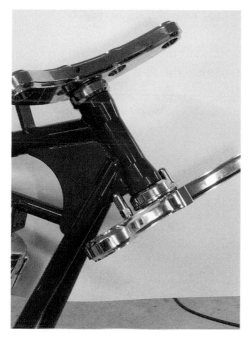

The regency trees are fully assembled and adjusted before the fork tubes are installed.

The neck bearings need to be packed with waterproof grease. It's important that the grease be worked up between the rollers - thus the small packing tool.

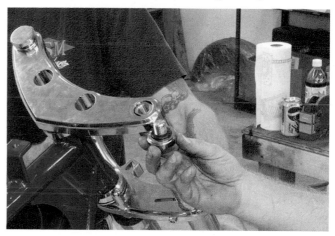

After the fork tubes are in place in the trees the top caps can be installed. Note the O-ring seal.

Billy pushes the tubes up into the trees, being careful not to scratch the chrome.

The engine was installed earlier. At this point the six-speed RevTech transmission is set in place on the transmission mounting plate.

Kendall holds the two wheel spacers, one for each side.

With the spacers in place the wheel can be set up into place and the lower right side cap installed. Cap nuts are nylon-collar type self-lockers.

You need to snug up the axle nut, then tighten the right side cap so the axle can't turn, then final tighten the axle nut to 50 ft lbs. Loctite is a good idea.

be final-bolted into the frame just behind the engine.

Next, Kendall installs the bearing races in the frame neck (note the tool in the photo), followed by the triple trees. Because these are special Regency trees designed by John Reed, the assembly is a little different from some others, as noted in the captions.

With the tapered bearings packed with waterproof grease Kendall slides the lower tree and stem up into the neck, adjusts the pre-load on the bearings and then installs the top triple tree.

While Kendall worked installing the bearing races and trees, Billy Manuel installed new seals in the fork's two lower legs, installed the fork dampers into the fork tubes and slid the tubes (the upper portion) down into the lower legs. An Allen bolt with a sealing washer under its head screws up from the lower leg into the damper rod and prevents the male and female fork sections from sliding apart. Once the two sides of the fork are assembled and filled with fork oil Billy slides them up into the triple trees and tightens the pinch bolts.

With the tubes in the triple trees, the top nuts with O-rings can be installed and tightened. Pinch bolts in the lower tree are tightened last.

INSTALL FRONT WHEEL AND BRAKE

The front wheel comes in a raw condition, meaning that the tire must be mounted, and the tapered wheel bearings set up, packed and installed (which is covered in the Biker's Choice section). Next, the single front brake rotor is installed on the wheel hub, then the two outer spacers can be installed, followed by the axle. Finally the front wheel can be slid up into place and tightened. It's important to follow the right sequence for installing the wheel and axle. In Kendall's shop they snug down the axle cap on right side fork leg and then install the nut on the left side. After tightening the large axle nut, the two nuts holding the axle cap in place can be final-tightened.

This bike uses a single front caliper, which is installed now, using the bolts and hardware that comes with the kit. It's important to use the right mounting bolts as the entire weight of the bike, multiplied by velocity, is transferred to the frame when you make a panic stop. As shown, thin shims that come with the caliper are used to center the caliper over the rotor.

Next to be installed is the six-speed transmission, at this point the nuts that screw onto the four main mounting studs are left only snug, not fully tight.

Before any of the primary components can be installed the stator for the alternator must be installed. The small Allen bolts that hold this in place are pre-treated with Loctite and should be tightened to 30 to 40 inch lbs. Now the boys put the small OD washer on the shaft, followed by the rotor or stator cover. Like most frames that run big rear tires, this one uses a spacer, with O-ring seal, between the engine and the inner primary.

The swingarm can't be installed until the final-drive belt is wrapped over the transmission sprocket. The boys also attach the shocks to the front mounts. Next, the swingarm snubbers or stops are installed (you don't want the shocks to act as the suspension stop). Installing the swingarm is pretty straight forward, though you should be sure to use Loctite on the big through bolts, which are tightened to 120 ft. lbs.

INNER PRIMARY AND PRIMARY DRIVE

Before the engine and transmission can be final-bolted in place, the inner primary must be assembled. This is one of the more confusing parts of the process, as there are "extra" parts shipped with the inner primary to cover multiple applications.

Two seals and a bearing must be pressed into place before the inner primary can be bolted in place: In Kendall's shop the main shaft seal must be pressed into place first, then the inner snap ring is squeezed with a set of snap-ring pliers and set into the lower groove. Finally the main shaft bearing is pressed into the inner primary housing followed by the outer snap ring. As a note, press-in means just that. It does not mean beat into place with a hammer and socket. The other seal that needs to be installed is the jackshaft seal for the starter.

Of note, a separate set of instructions comes

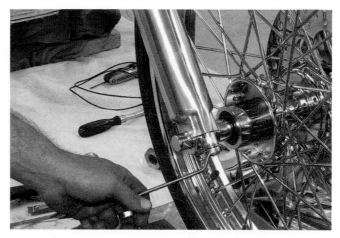

After the axle nut is tightened to the final torque spec, the right side cap nuts should be loosened (so the axle can seat itself) then final-tightened to 9 - 13 ft lbs.

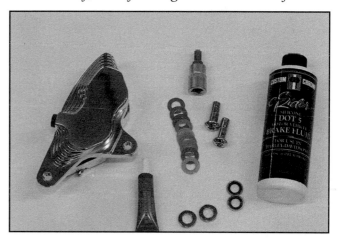

The kit comes with the front caliper, torx-type mounting bolts & driver, shims for positioning, washers for mounting and sealing washers for the line connection.

The nice thing about a kit - you know the caliper will fit. You do need to carefully position the caliper over the center of the rotor, however.

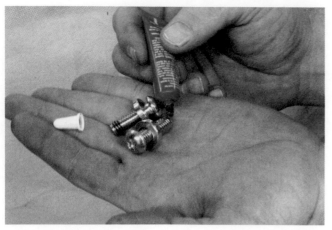

It's important to put blue locking compound on the caliper-mounting bolts before they're installed - you don't want these to back out of the hole.

Small Allen bolts are used to secure the stator to the engine case. Loctite should be used on the bolts (ours were pre-treated with locking compound).

Thin shims that come with the caliper are used between the caliper and the mounting on the lower leg to get the caliper centered over the rotor as shown.

A close up of the installed rotor. Note the electrical plug protruding from the case.

Charging circuit on a V-twin is pretty simple: one stator with a plug that slides through case, one regulator, one magnetic rotor/stator cover. Two washers not shown.

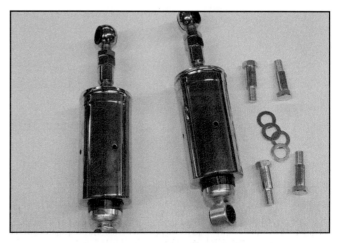

High quality and adjustable, these Progressive shocks came with our kit. Be sure to use the correct mounting bolts with Loctite.

with the inner primary. Or you can swallow your pride and take the whole she-bang down to the local shop.

Once the inner housing is tightened to the engine and transmission, the engine and then the transmission mounting bolts are final-tightened. In order to check the alignment of the engine and transmission the inner primary is taken off. Essentially the inner primary should slide on and off easily. If it doesn't then there is a problem with the engine and transmission alignment and one or the other (usually the transmission) must be shimmed.

Note: be sure the shocks are fully tight before the inner primary is installed for the last time.

Sometimes called the "fifth transmission stud" the right side transmission stud came very close to the right side shock body on this bike (see photos). Kendall simply used a small die grinder to cut a few threads off the stud with the transmission still in the frame. Option two would be to pull the transmission and cut the stud with the transmission out, or you could put in a bolt, though the threads in the housing are exposed to gear lube on the inside so any bolt you use needs to be coated with sealer.

Once the inner primary is installed for the last time the starter can be installed from the right side. The starter drive, a somewhat complex series of springs, shafts and couplers, is installed from the left side, per the photos (with possible help from a service manual).

The clutch hub and plates need to be assembled before the primary drive assembly is installed. Because the clutch assembly is spring loaded this is a job you might take down to the local V-twin shop. As shown in the photos, the primary drive is installed as an assembly, i.e., the chain with the front compensator assembly and the clutch assembly. Alignment is critical and must be checked after installation, per the photos. The nut that holds the clutch pack to the transmission shaft has left hand threads and should be tightened to 75 ft lbs. The compensator nut is tightened to 150 to 165 ft lbs.

Preventing the engine from turning over as

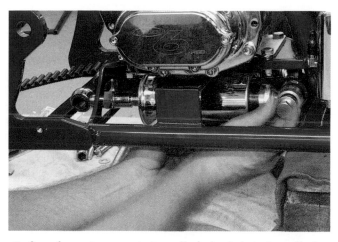

Before the swingarm is installed the belt is installed on the transmission pulley and the shocks are bolted up at the frame.

Shocks are meant to control the movement of the swingarm, not stop the movement. That's why it's important to put these rubber stops in place.

With the pivot bearings in place, the swingarm is slipped into place. In this design the belt is positioned between the frame and swingarm.

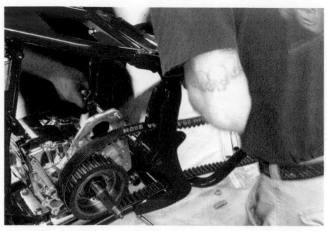

As Barry holds the swingarm and cross-shaft in position Jesse gets a pivot bolt started. Pivot bolt holes might have a paint build up and need cleaning.

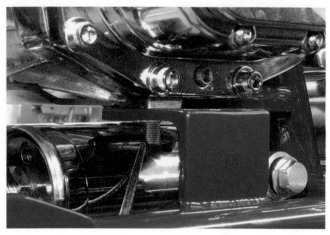

This is the "fifth transmission stud." A punch was used to point out the way this stud ended up too close to the body of the shock.

Inner primary comes as a kit requiring you to install things like the mainshaft seal and bearing, and the starter shaft bushing and seal.

you tighten the compensator nut can be done with a special tool illustrated in factory service manuals. Or simply wait until the rear brake is installed and bled and then lock the rear wheel with the brake pedal.

Installation of the forward controls is next, another pretty straightforward operation. They come with spacers to move them outboard. In the interest of keeping the bike narrow we chose to leave the spacers off though this can shorten the life of your new tennis shoes considerably (at least the right-side shoe). With the forward controls and kick stand bolted to the bike, it's time to install the handle bars. Note in the photos the trick way a piece of twine is pushed through the bars with compressed air so the wiring harness can be pulled through the bars before installation.

Installation of the headlight comes next. The only trick here is to use a good enough bolt as noted in the photo captions.

REAR WHEEL

Installation of the solid rear wheel is next. Like the front, the wheel comes raw, meaning you have to install bearings and spacers. The rear wheel pulley is installed, with a spacer between the wheel and the hub, that puts the pulley off to the left enough that the belt won't interfere with the left side of the tire. Allen bolts, coated with a little red Loctite, hold the pulley to wheel hub, these are tightened to 55 to 65 ft lbs.

Another set of button-head Allen bolts are used to secure the brake rotor to the right side of the wheel. These are coated with blue Loctite and tightened to 25-30 ft lbs.

Rear Wheel Install and align

Billy rolls the wheel up into place and wraps the belt over the pulley. Next the wheel is supported while the axle is inserted from the left side. As the axle is installed Billy holds the left side axle spacer in place, then pushes the axle through the wheel, out the other side, through a series of spacers and out the right side of the frame.

Ideally, alignment of the rear wheel and belt should be pretty simple. The position of the engine and transmission position is fixed. The left-side axle-spacer provided should position the wheel pulley directly behind the transmission pul-

The inner primary ships with more than one bushing, you need to choose the one that fits the hole in the housing, and the starter coupler in Barry's left hand.

Barry holds the inner primary so we can see the back side just before installation. You can see the installed seals for both the starter shaft and the main shaft.

Before and after inner primary housings.

The inner primary must be installed and tightened to the engine and transmission before the transmission-to-frame nuts are final-tightened.

Be sure to use an O-ring on either side of the primary spacer.

Once the engine and transmission are final-tighened the inner primary should slide on and off easily.

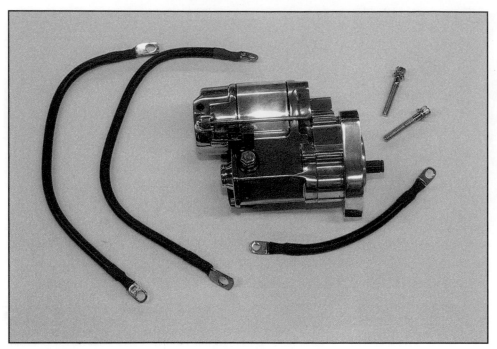

The foundation of the electrical system, one high torque starter, two battery cables and one engine-to-frame cable.

ley so the belt runs straight and true. On the right side of the hub there are three spacers used, an inner spacer that should protrude out slightly from the edge of the rotor, the caliper bracket, and the outer spacer between the caliper bracket and the frame.

The three right side "spacers" should fill the space between the hub and the frame, and leave the caliper bracket positioned so the caliper itself can be centered over the rotor.

Barry, who has extensive experience with these kits, reports that "sometimes the paint on the inside of the swingarm can cause the fitment to be off, but in all the kit's I've put together the spacing supplied was correct."

Like the front caliper kit, the rear comes with thin shims that can be used to position the caliper correctly over the exact center of the rotor.

INSTALLATION OF RIGHT SIDE TRANNY COVER, CLUTCH RELEASE MECHANISM AND CABLE

Clutch Cable and Linkage.

Installation of the clutch cable starts as Jesse installs the release plate, with the adjusting screw in place, into the center hub of the clutch hub. The adjusting screw can't be correctly set until the right side transmission cover and cable are installed. Thus, Jesse's next move is to screw the clutch

Once the inner primary is installed for the last time you can bolt up the starter motor to the back side.

cable into the transmission cover and attach the cable end to the ramp and coupler assembly inside the transmission cover. Now the transmission cover can be bolted into place and the Allen bolts tightened to 7 to 9 ft. lbs. The cable is now routed along the frame (being careful to avoid sharp bends) and up toward the handle bars. Kendall used two optional Arlen Ness cable stand-offs to aid in the neat routing of the cable. With the right side cover in place the initial clutch adjustment can be performed: The adjusting bolt located on the release plate should be screwed in by hand until you feel it touch the push rod, then backed of 1/4 turn, and locked in place with the lock nut.

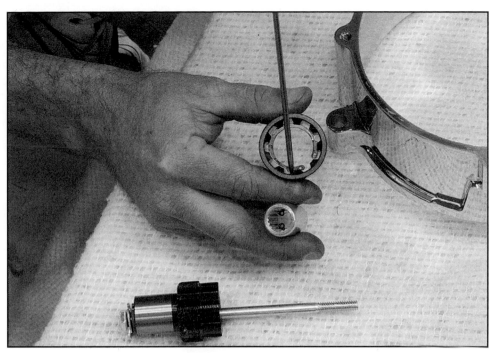

Here you can see the snap rings installed in both the jackshaft parts before installation.

The outer primary can be installed at this point though first the correct bushing must be installed (as shown in a series or earlier photos). The right bushing is the one that fits the recess in the cover and slides over the end of the starter drive.

BATTERY CABLES AND OIL TANK

Before installing the oil tank Kendall attaches two ground wires to the inner primary with the starter bolt, per the photos. Then the positive cable is attached at the big positive terminal on the starter. The shorter one goes from the starter bolt to the frame.

Installation of the oil tank is next, and once in

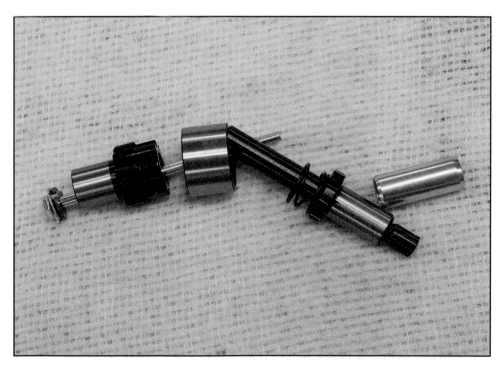

This blow up shows the various parts of the starter drive assembly. Be sure to coat them with a little oil before installation.

The parts that make up the chain-type primary drive. Clutch hub assembly on the right is under tension and may need to be assembled at a shop.

With the clutch hub nut and compensator assembly snug Jesse puts a straight-edge against the chain and checks the distance to the edge of the inner primary....

Offset compensator assembly comes with thin shims that can be used to align the primary drive (see photo at top right).

...then does the same thing just ahead of the clutch, the difference in the two readings should be no more than .014 inch.

Jesse slides the engine drive assembly up into place.

The "shoe" just above Jesse's thumb is raised or lowered to adjust the chain tension. When cold the up and down play should be 5/8 to 7/8 inch.

place the two battery cables are routed up into the battery box. Then the battery hold down strap is connected to the tab on the back of the oil tank.

SHEET METAL

Most custom bikes are built twice, once in the raw as a complete mock-up, and once for real after all the parts have been painted and polished. You don't want to be welding brackets on the frame, or enlarging a mounting hole, after all the parts are painted.

This situation is a little different, however. First, everything you need to assemble the bike is included, so there is no need to build brackets. Second, Custom Chrome has enough confidence in the jigs used to build the Santee frames that they recommend having the frame painted as soon as it comes out of the box.

As mentioned earlier, they do recommend doing a mock-up of the sheet metal. In the case of the front fender and the two tanks, it's necessary to make sure the parts all fit. Our kit came with two lower brackets for the Fat Bob Tanks, trial and error determined which one was the best fit.

The rear fender is more work as it comes as a blank and is not drilled. This trial fitting session is perhaps best explained by the photos. Essentially, you have to determine where the fender should mount. The idea is to make sure the fender looks right on the bike, meets the seat, and can't rub on the tire. Even when the suspension is bottomed out.

The license bracket is next. This is a trick custom piece designed by Rick Doss. Though many people prefer to have the taillight on the left side of the bike, this bracket, when used on the 250 frame, will only work on the right.

HANDLE BAR CONTROLS AND SWITCHES

One of the more challenging parts of this assembly business is the installation of the handle bar controls. It's one of those situations where it pays to take your time.

The switches and switch housings come pretty raw. There is one harness for each side of the bars, each harness has the switches hanging from one end. After you determine which harness goes to which side, you need to work the harnesses down

Jesse puts blue Loctite on the mounting bolts before installation. We inverted the shift lever so it would match the arch of the other side.

The kick stand mounts to the left side forward control.

Once the wires are pulled through the bars (see next page) Billy installs bushings in the top tree and then sets the bars in place.

The idea here is to get string run through the bars so it can be use to pull the two harnesses through.

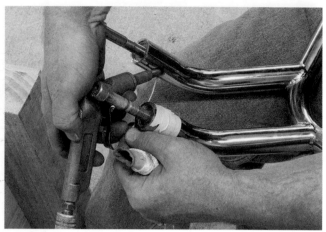

First, tie a big knot on the end of the string, tape off all the openings but two, insert the end with the knot and blow baby blow.......

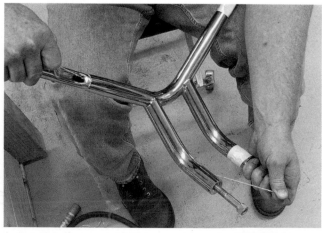

... the air pressure will carry the end with the knot out the other hole, as shown. Now do this again for the other side of the bars.

Kendall points out the Grade 8 bolt they use to mount the headlight, "the vibration tightens the bolt, a cheap one will break off."

After installing the bottom mounting bolt the headlight is "aimed" and the through bolt is tightened.

The top motor mount assembly, chrome plated of course, complete with the off-set bushing.

through the bars (part of this was covered earlier), install the switches into the housings and then install the housings on the bars. The right side is a bit more complex as that switch assembly includes the tension adjustment for the throttle and the two throttle cables.

More specifically, the kit comes with small screws, pre-treated with Loctite, that are used to hold the switch assemblies into the housings. On the right side, you have to install the tension screw part way into the lower housing, then install the very small C-clip so the tension screw can never fall out (this is harder than it sounds). Next you have to install the ramp that actually tensions the throttle.

The throttle cables use two different diameter housings so you can't get the wrong one in the wrong hole in the throttle housing. The cable with the spring end is the return cable. A small mini-clip in the handlebar end of each outer cable helps to hold the outer cable into the throttle housing. It's a good idea to lube the cables with liquid silicone or liquid graphite before installation. Kendall had to take the small mini-clips off and squeeze them with a small pliers so they would snap into the housing more easily.

With the switches in the switch housings, Kendall mounted the assembly loose on the bars, and began pulling the harness wires at the risers, to take the slack out of the wires and move the switches and housings closer to the center of the bars. In this way he gradually worked the switch housings up against the controls. It takes time to work through this and get everything to fit correctly.

Once the two cables are installed in the housing and the housing is installed on the right side of the bars, the two cables can be routed as shown and attached to the Mikuni carburetor.

With any cable, but the throttle cables in particular, it's important that they be routed neatly, with gentle bends so the cable can't be pinched and won't stick because they've been tied in a figure-8.

Once the throttle cables are attached and the switch housings are in place Kendall and Barry

The belt used here is 1-1/8th inch wide, slightly narrower than the original 1-1/2 inch examples. This makes more clearance for the rear tire.

Here you can see the axle partly installed and the left side axle spacer.

The screw driver points to the inner most of the three spacers.

Another view of the right side axle and the spacers.

The rear caliper comes with mounting bolts, shims and a can of silicone brake fluid, much like the front.

The right side spacers should leave the caliper bracket positioned so it's easy to center the caliper over the rotor.

connect and attach the clutch cable to the handlebar control. Once the cable end is secure in the lever and the lever is attached to the control, the final clutch adjustment can be made at the adjustment sleeve in the cable.

THROTTLE CABLES

Spray adhesive is used to glue the inner and outer grip together, then Kendall puts the grip on the right end of the bar. After taking the tank off, the cables are routed per the photos. The cable with the spring is the return cable, the small cable ends are placed on the carburetor end of the cables.

With both cables attached at the carburetor, Kendall lengthens each housing until he has adjusted the free play out of the throttle assembly. The throttle should work at this point without sticking.

Barry offers the following advice: "On the left side it's important to put the switch boxes up there first, and get all the wires in the dimple in the bar, you don't want to pinch a wire. And I tell guys to put the switch boxes on first. Otherwise they want to glue that grip on the bar, and sometimes they put the grip on so far it bottoms, then it's on too far and won't let the switch boxes mount correctly. Then you've almost got to destroy the grip to get the grip off."

Barry double checks the initial clutch adjustment after the cable is installed, there should be play in the cable at this point. After he's sure the initial clutch adjustment is correct he will go ahead and adjust the clutch cable.

About routing the clutch cable, Barry adds the following comments: "It's important to get a nice gradual sweep when you route the clutch cable, it makes for a better pull, you don't want to have any sharp turns in the cable, and I like to run the cable so it is above the cross braces on the frame, that way it can't hang down below the frame. Of course you have to keep it away from the exhaust. And it's important to have a little play in the cable, not in the handle because that may just be slop in that pin where the lever attaches. You need to pull back on the cable where it goes into the control and measure the play between the cable

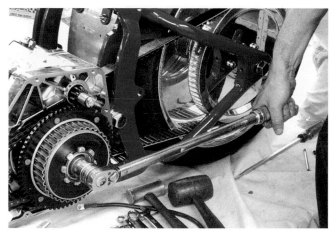

The clutch hub nut is left hand thread, tightened to 75 ft lbs. Do not over tighten.

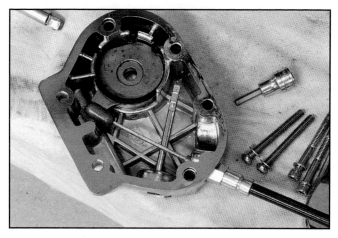

Cable is screwed into the housing (with an O-ring on the fitting) then ramp is set down on the balls and connected to the cable. Note position of snap ring.

Clutch release plate and adjusting screw are set in place and snap ring installed. The initial adjustment can't be made until the right side cover is installed.

With a gasket in place the right side cover can be installed....

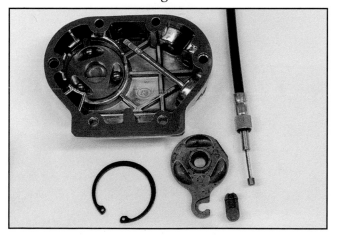

Right side tranny cover, clutch cable and ball-and-ramp assembly.

.... and the bolts tightened to 7 to 9 ft lbs. There is a "6-speed" cover that installs here as well.

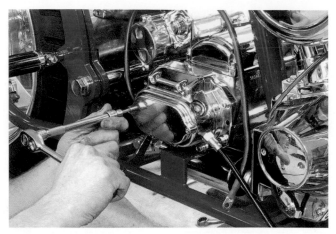

The last two transmission-cover bolts hold on the RevTech name plate.

With a new gasket in place Jesse puts the new outer primary in place. These bolts are tightened to 108 to 120 in. lbs.

Now the initial adjustment can be made, bolt is screwed in until it just touches the push rod, then backed out 1/4 turn and locked in place.

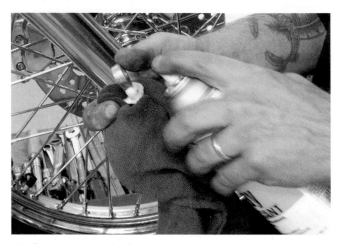

Before upper end of clutch cable is attached Barry works lube down between the cable and housing.

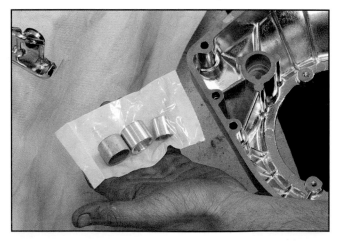

Before the outer primary can be installed the starter drive bushing must be installed per the instructions.

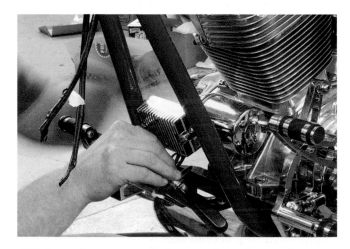

With the frame ground clean earlier, the regulator can be bolted in place. Two wires meet the stator-plug in the case, the other goes to the + battery terminal.

housing and the base of the control." (note the picture with the pointer).

WIRING

The harness kit that ships with the Goliath kit is from Thunder Heart and consists of five major components. There are four harnesses: one for each side of the handle bars, one front harness, and one rear harness. There is also one central harness controller. In addition there are a variety of connectors, tie-wraps and rolls of shrink wrap.

The information presented here is specific to the Thunder Heart kit. The details we provide may not help you with your specific wiring project, but they do provide an example of the kinds of organizing and patience that are required to do a good job of wiring a bike, no matter which harness kit is used.

Jesse starts by securing the base for the controller to the top tube between the tanks. The two handle bar harnesses have already been installed in the bars. These two groups of wires or harnesses, are run back near the control unit.

Wire the Terminal blocks

Each harness plugs into the central control unit. The trouble is, these plugs or terminal blocks are not attached to the ends of the individual harnesses. It's up to you (or who ever does the wiring) to install the plugs. This is actually a two-step process. First the individual wires have to be pushed through the back side of the plug (check the photos here to relieve confusion). Then the ends must be crimped on and then each wire can be pushed into the terminal block.

The wires, from a particular harness section, are pushed through the back part of the plug, making sure each wire with the correct color code is in the right spot. Once all the wires are in the correct location in the base of the plug, the small terminal ends can be crimped onto each individual wire. Then the wires, with terminal ends installed, can be snapped into the main terminal block.

The little one-way prongs on each terminal hold them in place. In fact, getting them back out of the terminal block can be difficult, so it's extra important you get them into the correct spot the first time.

A progress shot: At this point the engine, transmission, oil tank, and forward controls are installed, and the crew is ready to run the oil lines.

Here you can see how the cables come up into the battery box, and the tie-down strap.

This shot shows the two ground cables, one of which will go up into the battery box while the other goes to the frame (arrow).

51

Left side shows the motor mount assembly installed, along with the horn and choke cable. Primary housing will be sealed up shortly.

Clearance between the bracket and swingarm is tight, we had to "adjust" the bracket slightly. Positioning is also critical so the bracket won't hit the tire.

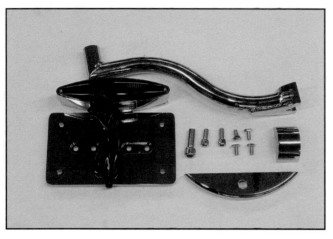

This Rick Doss taillight assembly mounts to the cross bar....

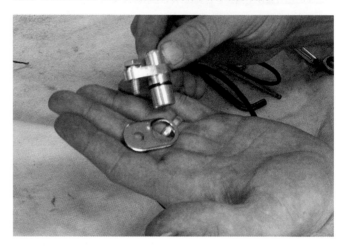

When the sensor is installed in six-speed transmissions the spacer (shown) must be used or the sensor will contact the gears inside the case.

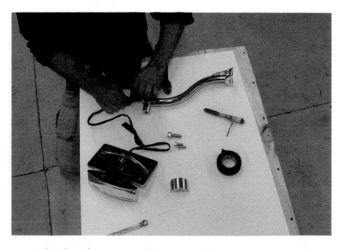

..... the hardest part of the installation is getting a piece of wire "fished" through the bracket and then pulling the small harness though the bracket.

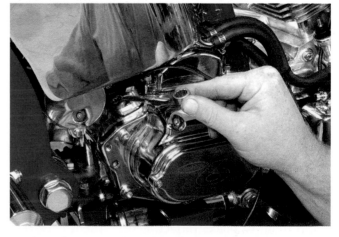

A short box wrench makes it easier to get at the 1/4 inch bolt used to secure the sensor and spacer in the transmission case.

Wires that are not used, like the turn signals on this bike, are wrapped into small groups and tie-wrapped to the frame for possible use later.

After the two front handlebar harness sections are crimped and plugged into the harness controller assembly, the rear harness section is plugged in and the wires are run toward the rear of the bike. There are 15 wires in this harness, (for things like oil pressure switch, brake light, taillight, solenoid, and neutral light).

Wiring Details

Jesse and Kendall group the wires according to their exact location and use. For example, all the wires for the tail and brake light are separated out and run into a piece of shrink tubing.

"Sometimes we run these wires through the frame," says Kendall, "but instead, we will run them up under the seat and then drill a hole and run them down under the seat. You have to be sure the seat isn't going to pinch the wires."

There are three wires coming out of the Rick Doss license/taillight bracket; one each for brake and taillight and one ground. Jesse runs the ground wire from this small harness to the battery negative, then tests the other two wires to determine which one operates the brake light and which one operates the taillight. Then he solders those two wires to the two wires identified earlier for the brake and taillight.

To solder the wires, Jesse strips off the insulation and twists the wires together and then applies liquid flux to clean the joint, before heating the connection and applying solder. The connection needs to be heated from underneath with the soldering iron until it's hot enough that the solder actually melts and is "absorbed" by the wires. In other words, you can't just get it warm and drool solder onto the connection. He cuts and slides shrink wrap tubing over each individual joint, (before twisting the wires together), then positions and heats the tubing after the soldering job is finished.

Ignition wiring

The best schematic of the ignition wires is included with the extensive packet of material that comes with the RevTech engine. Kendall forms a

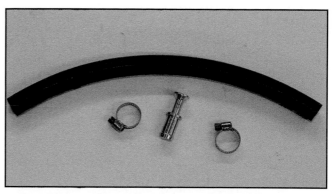

Though the oil lines have been routed, they still have to install the drain tube assembly...

....on the bottom of the oil tank.

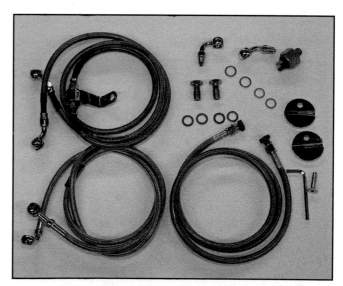

Rear brake-light switch (top right), screws into the fitting that is part of the mounting bracket.

As shown by the pointer, each banjo bolt is sealed by two copper or aluminum/neoprene sealing washers.

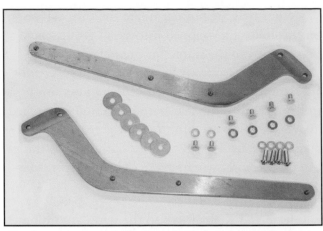

Fender struts are drilled so the bolts come in from the back side.

Some brake lines come with the fittings crimped to the line while others (like the front line shown here) come with separate fittings.

Struts are bolted on with two button-head Allen bolts, lock washers and heavy chrome washers.

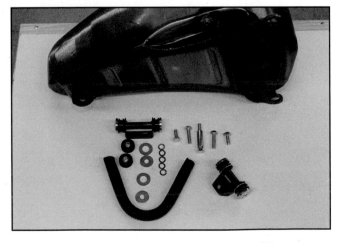

Tank mounting kit. Two tanks, upper and lower mounts, grommets and hardware.

You need to fit the fender so it: clears the tire, matches the radius of the tire/rim, and comes up snug under the seat.

small harness made up of the 5 wires from the module, plus the white with tracer wire from the rear section of the main harness. Note, some of the five wires from module are not used, in this case the wire for the tachometer and the wire for the VOES are not used.

The ignition that shipped with this engine will work in either single or dual-fire mode. The bike comes with a dual fire coil however, so that is how it's wired. There is no coil polarity in this dual fire mode.

To install the coil Barry puts two spacers behind the coil bracket, one thick and the other just a chrome washer, to space it out from the frame so it doesn't hit the rocker box.

Wiring for the ignition, which is made by Crane for CCI, is included in the information packet that comes with the complete RevTech engine.

Two wires from the various harnesses go to the positive battery terminal. One from the regulator (this wire feeds alternator power to the battery to keep it charged) and one from the rear section of the main harness (the power source for the ignition switch). "I leave these two wires long enough that they will fit either style of battery," explains Kendall, "regardless of the location of the terminals."

The light for the neutral light takes a special connector designed to slide over the stud on the transmission. For the starter a yellow connector with shrink collar is crimped and then shrunk over the correct wire.

Dash Wiring

The wire for the speedo runs up from the sensor on the transmission to the dash. The dash in turn has two small wiring plugs, one from the speedo and one from the indicator lights. The one from the speedometer has three wires in a small plug. Jesse cut the small plug off and put male/female plug-in terminals on either end instead. The larger of the two small plug ins, plugs into a slot on the main fuse block. All the dash connections must be fitted with plug-in connectors to ease removal of the dash for service.

The crimp connectors supplied with the kit

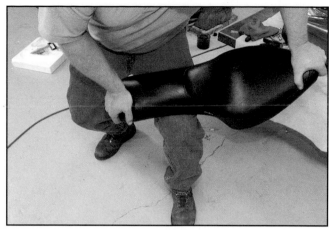

This seat base is made from metal, which allows Kendall to make some fine adjustments to the shape.

Hard to have too many clamps and vise grips. With everything clamped in place Kendall marks the outline of the struts on the fender.

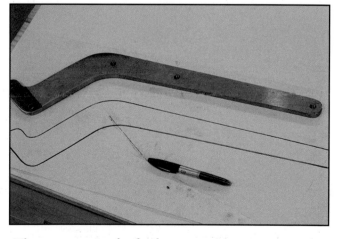

The next step in the fender-mounting sequence is to transfer the outline of the struts onto a piece of light board......

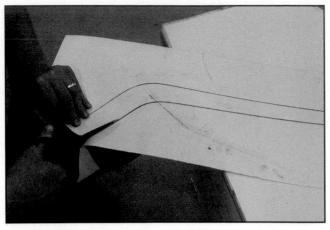

..... and cut out the silhouette of the strut before.....

The lower tank mount - our kit came un-drilled so Barry installed a threaded insert. Yours will probably be threaded, or you can use a through bolt and nut.

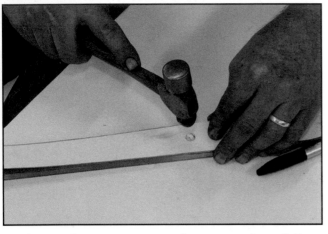

.....laying the new cutout on the strut and carefully "marking" the location of the holes (being careful not to damage the threads).

Here Kendall fits the left side gas tank. Note the washers under the top-rear frame mount.

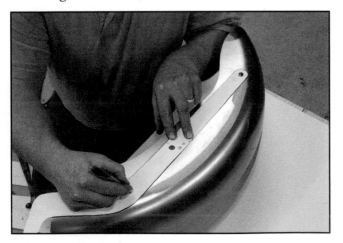

The final step before painting is to transfer the location of the holes to the fender, then drill the holes with a step drill.

Tank mock-up is really just a means of making sure the grommets meet the mounts and that all the mounts on the tanks are located correctly.

Handle bar switches come already attached to the ends of the two handle bar harnesses. Switches for each side must be attached to the housings.

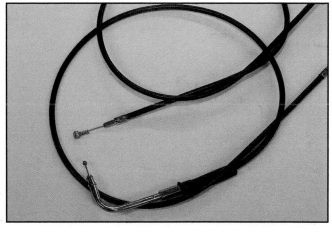

Most bikes use two cables, a pull and a return. The cable with the spring on the end is the return.

Close up shows the left side housing halves with the switches installed.

The cable housings are different diameters so you can't get the wrong cable in the wrong hole.

Both halves of the right side switch housing prior to installation of the throttle cables.

Both cables housings are installed, then the switch housings can be mounted to the bars.

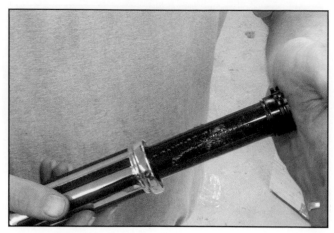

Contact cement is used to glue the grip to the throttle sleeve.

Close up shows the cables attached to the Mikuni carburetor. Cable in Kendall's hand, with the small spring, is the return (or close) cable.

Here you can see how the return cable end is attached to the carb, and how it installs in the bracket.

are great, and have built in heat shrink collars. Kendall forms a small two wire harness that goes to the rear brake light switch. Then puts a spade connector on each one.

To activate the battery Kendall runs it down to the local auto parts store to be filled with acid (acid is a hazardous material and did not ship with the kit). "They need to charge it with a trickle charger for 24 hours," explains Kendall. "Otherwise the battery gets a memory effect. If you only get it charged 60% the first time it will never go past 60%." Don't just let the store put a big charger on it for an hour and then put the battery in service."

A few more wiring details. The horn has two terminals, Jesse ran a short pigtail off one, put a round terminal on the end and grounded it to one of the bolts for the horn bracket. The other goes to the correct wire in the harness.

Three wires come up to the ignition switch, one from the battery, one for the ignition and one accessory wire. The terminals on the switch are close together so it's important to use insulated female spade terminals so there is no unintended connection between the terminals.

FINAL SHEET METAL

During the time Jesse and the crew were working on the wiring the sheet metal came back from the painter. As we said before, installation of the front fender is a no-brainer. Just be sure to use some Loctite on the nuts because you really don't want the fender to fall down on the tire while you're going down the highway.

When you get ready to mount the gas tanks (or do the mock-up of the sheet metal) you will find there are two different lower brackets with the kit. The one we chose wasn't tapped so Barry had to drill it out and install a threaded insert (we could have used a long through bolt but that seemed sloppy). Because the Goliath kit we assembled was an early one, we don't expect anyone else to have exactly the same trouble we did. And even after the lower mount was tapped, we had a little trouble getting the bolts to thread into the mount. All this points out the importance of the mock up stage – which we cut short in order to get the bike

The finished right side assembly. Throttle cable adjusters (to take the slack out of the cables) are hidden under the rubber covers.

With lever in place Barry adjusts the clutch with the threaded sleeve on the cable housing. There should be 1/8 inch of play between the ferrule and the housing.

The routing of the throttle cables was eventually changed from that shown here, note the later photos.

Here you can see how the coil mounts just under the seat.

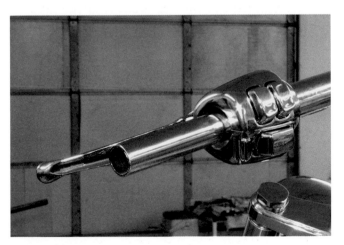

Left side grip can be installed, with contact cement, only after the switch housings are installed on the bars.

The wiring gets under way after Jesse attaches the main controller to the top frame tube.

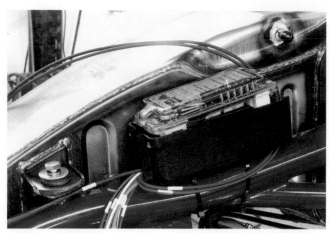

Here you can see the main controller in place on the top tube with wires separated out into logical groupings.

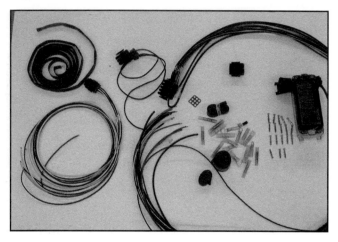

Wiring kit consists of main controller, four harnesses (two are already in the bars) and generous amounts of crimp tubes, terminals and shrink-wrap

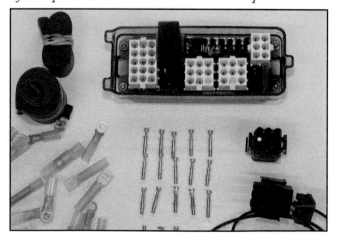

Close up shows the controller from the bottom. The four harnesses plug into the four white terminal blocks shown here.

built on a very tight deadline. When installing the grommets in the tank mounting points a little silicone spray helps the grommets slide into the bungs on the tanks (try not to get silicone on parts that aren't painted yet, any residue left after cleaning will cause imperfections in the paint).

Installation of the rear fender is likewise straight forward. The holes were drilled earlier prior to paint. So it's really just a matter of screwing the fine-threaded bolts in from the backside, into the fender struts, then installing the whole assembly on the bike.

DASH MOUNTING

After all the connections have been made and a cross over gas hose installed between the two tanks Jesse installs the aluminum support bracket that supports the front of the dash. For the rear of the dash there is no support bracket or hole in the frame. Barry explains, "you have to drill a hole in the frame and tap it."

Jesse puts a bolt in the front dash mounting hole to locate the dash, then figures out where the hole should go for the rear dash mount, then drills the hole and taps it.

PIPES AND MISCELLANEOUS

When it comes time to install the pipes, Kendall explains that there are two styles of gaskets that can be used between the pipes and the heads; "the smaller gaskets make more horsepower, they're less restrictive, but they are harder to install. You have to be sure the face of the pipe, where it goes up into the head, seats up nice and even against the gasket."

There are holes in the frame, just under the swingarm pivot on the right, tapped for the bolts that screw into the brackets for the exhaust. The inside of the pipes, at the head end, are sprayed with high temp spray paint to minimize bluing.

ADJUST SHOCKS AND CHECK TIRE CLEARANCE

Though the clearance between the tire and the fender was checked during the mock up phase, it's a good idea to check it one more time. So Kendall drops the shocks and lifts the swingarm up ALL the way, to make sure there's no way the tire can hit the inside of the fender or the stud for the

These are the two harness from the bars, with the wires pushed through the back side of the terminal block (controller was removed for this shot).

Here you can see the left side tank installed and the way the throttle cables were eventually routed.

Kyle Never applied four coats of the special-mix urethane then covered it all with four coats of urethane clear using Sikkens materials.

After finding the right gasket Kendall installs the petcock on the left-side tank.

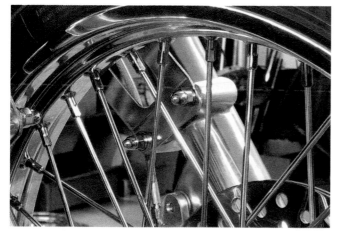

Acorn nuts (these came with the kit) with a drop of Loctite are used to neatly install the front fender.

Bolts for one side are tightened after all three are started. Pipe inside the fender is for routing the taillight wire - in a different application.

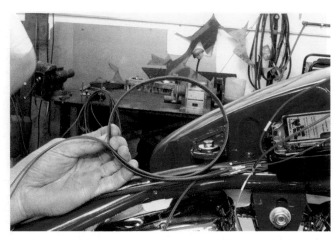

Wires for tail and brakelight, ignition, and the brake light switch are separated out of the bundle of wires and grouped together in shrink wrap.

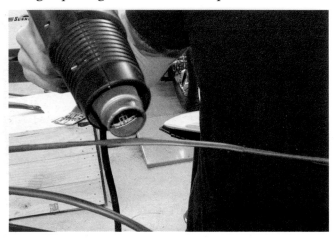

The term "shrink wrap" tells the whole story. Just pick the right size shrink wrap, slide the wires inside and apply heat.

Ignition wires are included in this harness. 4 wires come from the ignition module under the cam cover, white wire with tracer comes from the rear harness.

the bracket and created more clearance by bending the bracket slightly but it's hard to do without nicking the frame or swingarm with the long adjustment tool. Barry says this is only an issue with the 250 rear tire.

#2. The hoses coming off the oil tank hit the rear exhaust pipe. Fixing these was simple, Kendall simply bent the nipples.

#3. As mentioned, bleeding the brakes (especially the front) required great patience.

#4. Wiring. We had a couple of little snags with the wiring. First, there was no power to the solenoid, due to the fact that the small pins in the terminal blocks backed out when the block was plugged into the control unit. This was caused primarily by the fact that the crimps were not as neat as they could have been because we did not have a high quality crimping tool like the one shown.

#5. The left front fork tube leaked at the bolt that screws in from the bottom, requiring only that the bolt be tightened to put more pressure on the sealing washer. Jesse reports that sometimes they put teflon tape on the threads of these bolts.

#6. The exhaust pipes didn't run parallel, which requires only a little adjustment by Jesse.

When asked whether our troubles are typical with scratch built bikes, Jesse replies that there are three major areas where people have trouble: "They have trouble with the brakes because they just throw the calipers on there and don't realize they have to use the spacers. The other problem area is primary chain spacing, they aren't careful about that. And they have trouble with the wiring.

Q&A: PHIL MICKELS ON BUILDING A BIKE FROM SCRATCH.

Phil Mickels recently built a stretched rubber mount bike using the Daytec 180 Episode frame. Though Phil did not work from a bike kit, he did build a motorcycle from scratch. This puts him in a position to share what he learned as a first-time builder with the rest of us. We asked him to explain what he learned along the way and what kinds of advice he would pass along to anyone

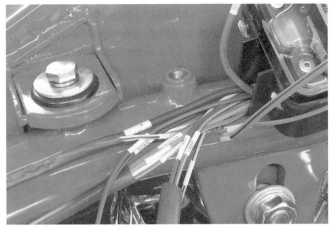

Here you can see how the wires from the "rear" harness have been sub-divided into smaller harnesses. Note: labels are not enclosed in shrink wrap.

This is the clutch adjusting sleeve. We removed the rubber boot and then used clamps to neatly route the cable along the frame.

These two wires go to the rear brake light switch, which was later moved behind the transmission.

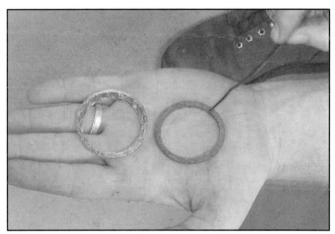

Exhaust gaskets come in two versions, the smaller version seen on the right is less restrictive and allows the engine to make more power.

The 16-size batteries come in two terminal layouts. Wires that run to plus and minus posts are long enough to reach either side of the battery box.

This shot shows the tanks in place with the top cross-over tube, and the dash just before final mounting. Note the towel used to protect the paint.

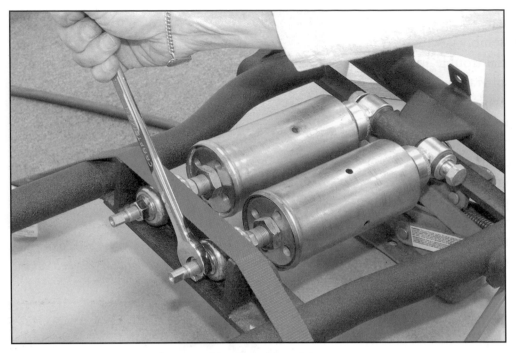

These post 2000 soft-tail shocks attach as shown. The threaded collar seen on the shock body makes it possible to adjust the length of the shock and thus the ride height.

Once the shocks are in place Skeeter can set the TC 88B style transmission case in place.

THE KIT INCLUDES

The heart of this kit is the frame and swingarm from Rolling Thunder designed for right side drive. As shipped, this frame comes with what might be called non-radical specifications: two inches of stretch and a neck set at thirty eight degrees. This is not a chopper with stretched downtubes and a raised neck but rather a stylish cruiser with a modern silhouette.

The billet triple trees come with the kit, as do the large diameter 46mm Paioli fork legs. Between the fork tubes is a 130/70X18 Avon tire on a cast aluminum wheel. At the other end of the bike is the ultra fat 250/40X18 Avon tire and another cast wheel with the same design as that seen on the front.

The Biker's Choice kit includes all the sheet metal, including Perewitz stretched fat bob gas tanks, horse shoe style oil tank, the wide rear fender with struts and the wrap around front fender. Fasteners are not included in this kit.

Unlike some others, this kit does not come with engine, transmission, brakes, wiring harness, mirrors or taillight

The sleeve nut will only go into one end of the left side spacer. The right side spacer must also be positioned as shown in the top photo.

The through bolt and one sleeve nut slides in from the right; through the spacer, through the transmission tail section, and the left side spacer.

This mock up shot shows how the right side spacer slips into the recess on the swingarm.

How deep the sleeve nut screws onto the cross shaft can be measured as shown, the amount of threads engaged should be the same from one side to the other.

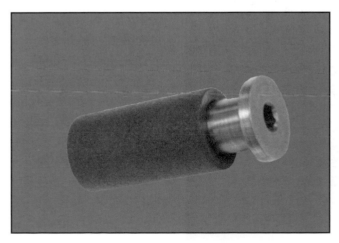

Close up shows one spacer and the sleeve nut. Both spacers are machined so they will accept the sleeve-nut in only one end.

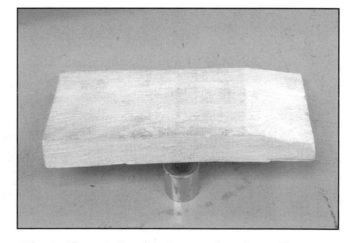

This is Skeeter's "wedgie," a very handy small ramp useful for propping engine or transmission into just the right position during installation.

73

This is what the engine and transmission look like when both are correctly installed in the frame.

This shot of the bottom of the neck (with the collar held in place) shows how the fork stop collar interacts with the tab on the frame.

With the collar positioned on the lower tree Skeeter marks the position of each hole.

Things get under way as Skeeter sets the swingarm in place behind the frame and installs the two shock absorbers. These late model soft-tail shocks use an eye at one end and a threaded stud at the other, unlike earlier shocks that mounted with an eye at either end. A threaded section on the body of these particular shocks allows you to easily adjust the bike's ride height.

INSTALL ENGINE AND TRANSMISSION

The swingarm pivot bolt goes through the tail end of the transmission housing so the transmission must be set into the frame before the pivot bolt and bushings are installed. The exact sequence of bolt and bushings is best illustrated by the photographs.

The cross shaft slides in from the right side. Skeeter uses a unique tool that he calls a "wedgie" (see photos) to prop the transmission up and hold it at the right level. This frame uses

A drill press is a handy thing to have when drilling these holes. Drill size is determined by the size of the tap.

a sleeve nut on either end of the cross shaft. The left side sleeve nut will only go in if the spacer on that side is positioned correctly. Once the cross shaft and nuts are in place, it's important to make sure each sleeve nut engages the same number of threads (see photo). Skeeter recommends waiting to fully tighten the sleeve nuts (to 90 – 110 ft lbs) until both the engine and transmission are installed and hanging on the mounting axles.

With help from George the engine is set into the frame and onto the 2X4s that support the chassis. Now the four bolts that connect engine to transmission can be installed and tightened. Oops, we forgot to install the belt, which means loosening the four engine-to-tranny bolts and removing the cross shaft so Skeeter can slide the swingarm back and then slip the belt in place. Final torque on the engine to transmission bolts is 30 – 35 ft lbs.

The wedge is used again to raise the front of the engine enough that the mounting axles can be installed. Like the sleeve nut used on the rear cross-shaft, the sleeve nuts used on the front motor mount axles are threaded all the way through and must be threaded onto the axle shafts the same amount on each end. Final torque for the engine mounting bolts is 70 to 80 ft. lbs.

INSTALL TRIPLE TREES

While some frame and triple tree combinations use big threaded studs screwed into the lower tree as fork stops, this example uses a neater way of accomplishing the same thing. A notched collar - attached to the lower triple tree – limits fork travel by interacting with a tab on the bottom of the neck.

Before the triple trees can be installed on the frame however, the fork stop collar must be installed on the lower tree. This is a relatively simple matter of drilling and tapping the holes in the aluminum triple tree (check the photos). The screws used to hold the collar in place are taper-head 10X24 machine screws, 1/2 inch

Once the holes are drilled, the tap can be used - very carefully - to cut the threads.

Here's the collar attached to the lower triple tree. This is a demo frame and only two screws were used to secure the collar to the tree.

Once the collar is in place the bearing can be pushed onto the stem of the triple tree. Normally this bearing would be packed with grease.

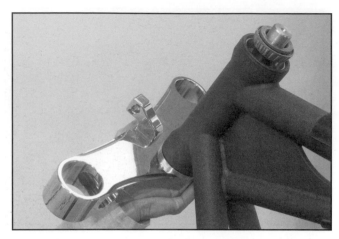

Once the stem is set into the lower triple tree, the assembly is slipped up into the neck.

Close up shows the cam-lock mechanism that pinches the tubes and holds them in place in the upper and lower triple tree.

long. The size of the drill used to drill the aluminum prior to the tapping is determined by the chart that comes with every tap set. You do need to use caution in any tapping operation, but especially when tapping aluminum. If the tap gets stuck or breaks off in the hole (horror of horrors) you are a screwed dude. It's much easier to simply use the right drill and tap very carefully. Skeeter recommends using lubricant while taping, and backing the tap out of the hole often to clean out the chips.

Once the collar is in place, the stem and then the lower tapered bearing, are installed. (The stem is attached to the lower tree with lock screws.) At this point Skeeter sets the lower tree and stem assembly up into the neck. Next he slides the fork tube assemblies into the lower tree and keeps them there by tightening the cam-locks so they are just snug and not fully tight. Now the top tree can be set in place and adjusted so the bearings are snug - or close to the final adjustment explained in the service manual. The tube assemblies are now adjusted up and down until the top of the tube is flush with the upper surface of the top tree. At this point the cam locks in both the upper and lower trees can be fully tightened.

After the tubes are set up into the lower tree, the top tree can be set in place.

This triple-tree design uses a nut on the top tree to adjust the tapered neck bearings. Once you're sure the bearings are adjusted correctly, which requires that the wheel be mounted and the front wheel be up off the ground, the adjusting nut is locked in place with an Allen bolt that screws through the upper tree.

It's time now to install the front wheel but first we need to install the tapered wheel bearings and set the end play – all of which is covered in the nearby side-bar on wheel bearings.

Installing the front wheel is pretty basic. Equal length spacers are used on each side, per the photo, to center the wheel between the fork legs. These spacers are shipped with the kit. Like the swingarm pivot shaft, the front axle uses sleeve-nuts on either end. You need to get the axle and spacers in place between the fork legs, then snug up one sleeve nut, clamp that nut in the lower fork leg (check the photos) then tighten the sleeve nut on the other side to factory specs of 45 to 50 ft. lbs., then tighten that sleeve nut in that lower leg (this is not as confusing as it sounds).

REAR WHEEL INSTALL

Before installing the rear wheel the pulley must be bolted to the hub. Bolts for this are provided with the kit and no spacer is needed

Next the adjusting nut is snugged down. Final adjustment is done after the wheel is on the bike. Note the small Allen bolt used to lock the nut.

Cam-locks are two-piece affairs. The other "half" is in the tree. and must be installed before the tube goes up into place.

Experienced builders often install the fork and wheel first so the bike can be clamped in place on the hoist. Front wheel installation is shown in the next sequence.

Wheel Bearings

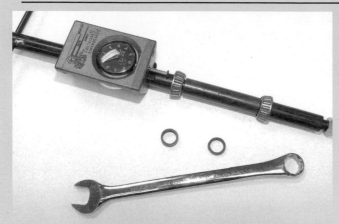

Shown is the Check Mate tool with tapered bearings and bearing spacer mounted.

To check end play the tool is inserted in the wheel, with bearings, spacer and any shims deemed necessary.

After torquing the nut to factory specs and bottoming the tool in one direction, zero the dial indicator, pull the tool in the other direction and read the end play.

The focus of this side-bar is an examination of the two types of wheel bearings found in most American V-Twins, the adjustment of the standard tapered-style wheel bearings, and the use of a nifty tool found in the Biker's Choice catalog.

BEARINGS IN GENERAL

Wheel bearings for aftermarket V-twins come in two varieties, tapered and sealed. Tapered bearings (sometimes called Timken bearings, though Timken is a trade name) are used on the front wheel seen in this Biker's Choice kit, and on both ends of many factory V-Twins built before the year 2000. These bearings need to be correctly adjusted for end play and lubricated on a regular basis (most manuals call for inspection and re-packing every 10,000 miles).

SEALED BEARINGS

Post-2000 Harley-Davidsons are equipped with sealed roller bearings that no longer need to be adjusted for end play or re-packed on a regular basis. These sealed bearings come in two sizes designed to fit either a 3/4 or 1 inch axle. The smaller axles are used on the front of most post-2000 factory bikes, and the rear of most post-2000 non-Dressers. Bikes that use a Dresser chassis, use the larger axle in the rear. Aftermarket wheels are likewise converting to the sealed bearings. In particular, most of the wide rear wheels designed for 230 and 250 tires are designed to accept the larger, 1 inch axle.

TAPERED BEARINGS
ADJUSTING THE END PLAY

Tapered bearings need to be installed with the correct amount of end play. Too much and the handling is affected, too little and the bearing life is shortened. Skeeter Todd recommends .002 to .006 inches as the correct end play for this tapered bearing installation (specifications vary to some degree by model and wheel). End play is determined by the length of the spacer used between the two bearings. A longer spacer (or the

Wheel Bearings

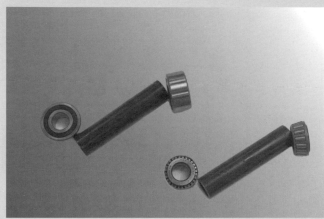

Two styles of bearing in common use, the sealed roller bearing on top and the tapered "Timken" type bearing on the bottom.

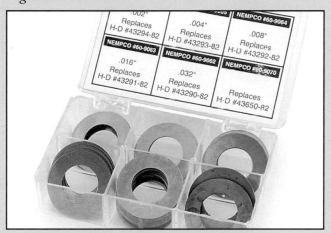

This kit from Biker's Choice (#41-0006) includes a mix of shims from .002 to.032 inches.

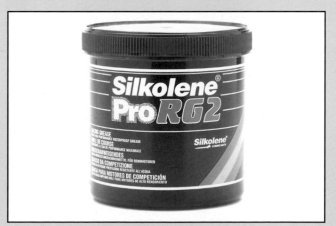

This high performance, waterproof grease is recommended for wheel bearings but could also be used for neck bearings.

addition of shims) will add to the end play while a shorter spacer will reduce the end-play measurement. A variety pack of shims is sold by Biker's Choice and most aftermarket outlets to make it easy to get the exact end play measurement you need.

In most cases the wheel must be mounted on the bike, or on an axle mounted in a vise, in order to check the end play. Once mounted the end play is checked with a dial indicator. This is obviously a hassle, especially in the case of a new wheel and bearing combination where you are starting from scratch. The tool shown here from Performance Specialties makes it easy to set up the end play on a new wheel without installing the wheel in the fork five or six times.

CHECK MATE TOOL

The Check Mate tool takes the place of the axle and has a dial indicator already mounted on the handle. Use of the tool is pretty simple. Just insert the tool through the wheel hub with bearings and the center spacer(s) you think is correct. Tighten the nut to the correct axle torque (55 ft. lbs. in this case). Push the tool all the way in one direction, zero the dial. Now pull the tool the other direction and read the end play on the large-diameter dial.

A suggested retail price of nearly $400.00 makes the tool a bit rich for a home shop, though the ease of use might make it a logical purchase for even a small service shop.

DON'T FORGET TO PACK 'EM

When setting up a wheel for the first time, it's obviously important to correctly pack the new bearings. This doesn't mean just slopping the bearing and hub with an abundance of wheel bearing grease, but rather, forcing grease up between each roller. If in doubt take the bearing to a shop, most of which have a special tool for packing tapered wheel bearings.

The kit comes with a variety of spacers, though it is up to you to find two two identical examples that will put the wheel in the center of the fork.

The idea is to get the wheel centered between the fork legs.

With the wheel in place Skeeter gets ready to slide the axle in from the left side.

Pinch bolts are used to clamp the sleeve-nuts in place in the lower fork, per the sequence described in the text.

Close up shows the spacer in place and Skeeter positioning the washer between the spacer and the inside of the fork.

The process of installing the rear wheel begins as Skeeter bolts the pulley to the hub.

between the pulley and the wheel to correctly position the pulley and ultimately the belt.

Skeeter begins the process of correctly locating the wheel in the frame by setting the wheel and axle in place, with no spacers. Next, he does a rough adjustment of belt tension and wheel placement fore and aft. "I'm trying to find out where the belt is happy," explains Skeeter. "The belt should run in a forward direction (as you spin the wheel) without crowding up against the edge of either pulley."

Once the wheel appears to be positioned correctly in the frame, Skeeter puts on the fender struts and then checks to ensure the struts are square to the frame and each other. "You can put a spacer under one of the mounting points for the struts to get the struts square. You can also move the struts out slightly from the frame to spread the fender slightly" (note the photos).

With the struts square on the frame you need to decide if the wheel is centered in the frame relative to the struts and fender. If not, and if there is room on the front pulley, you can move the wheel over slightly to get it centered between the struts.

In this case the wheel is very close to the left side strut. So Skeeter measures for the spacers per the side bar. To move the wheel to the right slightly he adds .125 inch to the left side spacer and subtracts

The hub-pulley-tire combination puts the inside edge of the pulley just outside the outside of the tire.

To set the belt tension and position the wheel in the swingarm Skeeter measures from the pivot to the axle centerline.....

Rear Brake Install

The rear brake caliper support and linkage rod can be mounted above the axle as shown, or.....

...then subtracts the width of the frame.

...below the axle as seen here. In either case, it's a good idea to keep the forward end of the torque rod as far forward as possible.

Before you measure for left side spacer, you have to know where the caliper bracket will ride. Inside spacer fits between bracket and outside of bearing.

To measure for the right side spacer, Skeeter determines distance from outside of frame to outside of the wheel bearing...

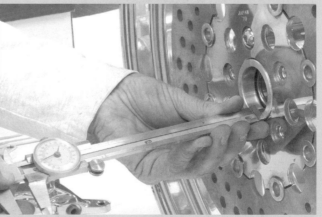

It is sometimes easier to measure from outside of bearing to outside of hub (as shown), then from outside or hub to inside of caliper bracket.

Rear Brake Install

When it comes to mounting the rear wheel and brake caliper, there are at least two things to be determined. First, you have to decide on the layout for the rear brake and where to mount the tab for the caliper-support rod. Second, you have to determine the exact position of the wheel, in a side-to-side sense, and then calculate the size of the necessary spacers.

When determining the layout for the caliper and support rod, Skeeter explains that you can mount the caliper either above or below the axle but that, "it's better to keep the support rod longer and attach it closer to the swingarm pivot, that way the braking forces will be fed to the frame and not to the swingarm."

With the wheel positioned in the frame as described in the text, Skeeter starts measuring for spacers on either side. On the right side, he measures the distance from the outside of the frame to the outside of the wheel bearing already placed in the wheel hub. Next, he measures the thickness of the frame. The thickness of the spacer equals the first dimension minus the thickness of the frame.

The left side is a little more complex as there are two spacers to buy or manufacture. You have to start by deciding where the caliper support

bracket should be positioned on the axle in order to position the caliper over the center of the rotor. The first spacer extends from the outside of the bearing, already positioned in the hub, to the inside of the caliper bracket. The other left-side spacer fits between the outsider of the caliper support bracket and the inside of the frame.

To make things just a little more confusing, Skeeter decided that the wheel should be moved over .125 inches to the right. So, in this case, it's necessary to subtract .125 inch from the right side spacer and add that to the outside spacer (the one used between the caliper bracket and the frame) on the left. The end result is a rear wheel that's centered under the fender, driven by a belt that runs in the center of the rear-wheel pulley.

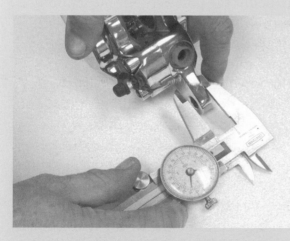

When setting all this up, you're going to have to figure out where to position the caliper bracket so the caliper itself will be centered over the rotor.

The ideal is a tire that's positioned in the center of the frame and a belt that's perfectly aligned with the front pulley.

.125 inch from the right side spacer. Of note, the axle is one inch in diameter, spacers do not currently ship with the kit.

SHEET METAL INSTALL

Installation of the wrap around oil tank is pretty straight forward. Essentially, the tank comes up from underneath. Once in place Skeeter swings out the top mounting tabs and installs the bolts. The way the mounting system for the tank is designed, there's plenty of opportu-

.....on both sides of the bike. There are no registration marks on the swingarm.

nity to adjust the exact position of the tank once it's hanging in the frame. As Skeeter explains, "I try to get it to match the lines of the frame, to get an even gap all the way around between the tank and the frame."

The post-2000 soft-tail frames use the center post mostly as a place to mount the coil. With the engine and transmission in place it's time to mount the post between the transmission case and the top frame tubes.

Though the kit does not include things like grips or mirrors, the forward controls *are* included. Installation is pretty simple, remember to put a little blue Loctite on the threads of the mounting bolts. The standard-issue kick stand bolts to the left side forward control.

As we stated earlier, the use of the TC 88B engine and tranny means that the inner primary is no longer called upon to determine the alignment of the engine and transmission. The inner primary can simply be installed with minimal trouble and no spacers. Because this bike is headed for a Biker's Choice display stand

To check the wheel position Skeeter spins the rear wheel in a forward direction and checks to see if the belt crowds up against either edge of the pulley

Skeeter installs the outer primary without installing the primary drive assembly.

The gas tanks mount in standard fashion, after the rubber grommets are installed at each mounting point. The position of the fender struts was determined earlier, at this point it's just a matter of bolting the fender to the struts and installing the whole thing on the frame with a spacer used at one mounting point (check the photos) to ensure the struts are square.

After the rear fender is installed Skeeter takes a minute for an important step: First the shocks are disconnected from the frame and then the rear suspension is fully bottomed to check for interference between the fat tire and the fender or mounting hardware.

The handle bars and controls were pre-assembled on the bench earlier so now it's just a matter of dropping the bushings into the top triple tree, setting the bars in place and then running the mounting bolts up from underneath. Note, it's a good idea to run a tap up into the threads on the bottom of the bars.

The front fender is installed last because, as Skeeter explains, "I've seen too many people put the front fender on early in the project, then drop a bolt or a wrench and put a big chip in the new paint job."

The fender spacers come with the kit and are used between the fender and the fork legs. The bolts used to mount the fenders screw through from inside, with a washer under the head and blue Loctite on the threads.

At this point the mock-up is finished. Anyone working in their own shop would spend time examining the bike for any flaws, and to ensure the rear fender position is correct, before disassembling the whole thing for paint.

After the "spin test" the belt should be in the center of the pulley and not crowded up against either edge.

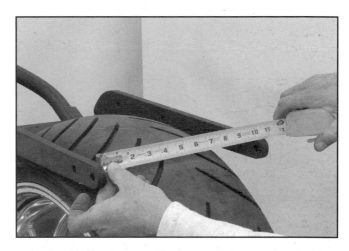

The fender struts must be far enough apart and parallel to each other.

To make sure they are parallel, Skeeter checks the dimension taken at the front with that taken at the rear of the struts.

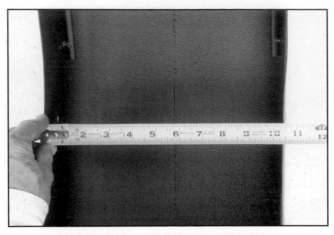

Sometimes the fenders are sucked-in in the center. The struts must be positioned to pull the sides out and ensure the fender can't touch the tire.

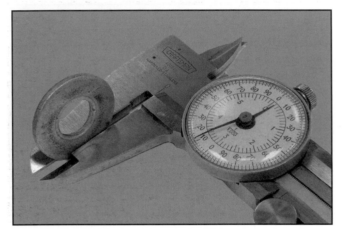

In order to get the struts parallel Skeeter measures a series of shims.....

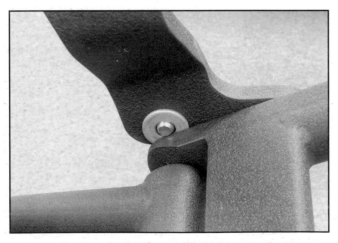

..... and places one between the left side strut and the frame. A small shim makes a sizable difference at the end of the strut.

INTERVIEW WITH SKEETER TODD FROM BIKER'S CHOICE

Skeeter Todd hasn't always been in the motorcycle business. For many years Skeeter worked construction. In fact, Skeeter helped build the stretch of freeway that connects Albany New York, location of his Biker's Choice office, and the small town an hour west of Albany where he lives. But, as Skeeter explains, "Even before I started working with Biker's Choice I always built Harleys in the garage at night." Today, Skeeter's garage is filled with a variety of interesting projects. There's the Harley flathead motor mated to a five-sped transmission, set in a modern frame, and next to that a blown big-block Chevy engine on a stand (the next engine for Skeeter and Marie's boat). Then there are the complete and running bikes. XRs, CRs, FXRs and some that defy easy description. Near the door is the daily driver, a test-mule Dresser equipped with turbo.

For Skeeter, the best bikes are the ones that work. Bikes you can hustle down a twisty road or simply use as fun, reliable transportation. As product specialist for Biker's Choice, all the new parts destined for the catalog must first be approved by Skeeter. His desk (assuming there's a desk underneath all that stuff) and the floor around it are littered with everything from billet wheels to new brake line fittings. Among all those prototype parts, the ones that Skeeter describes with glee, the ones he fights for in product meetings, are the innovative designs. The "better idea" parts that will make a motorcycle faster or safer, or make life easier for people who modify and build motorcycles. Skeeter Todd is a motorcycle nut — working to make life easier and more interesting for the rest of us.

Skeeter, tell us what you see as the advantage of selling a kit, and why Biker's Choice developed the Bike in a Box product line?

The average guy can't just pick parts from the catalog and then take them back if the tire is too big or two small, or the fork tubes are too long or too short. The kits are designed to help the average guy so he knows what the profile of the bike will be before he starts. The silhouette is pre-determined. He or she knows the bike will have the right look without buying two front ends. It's a customer convenience. My frame rails are up 3 degrees, the fork tubes are the right length. The pieces that determine the overall look are already chosen.

What are the advantages of right side drive?

For situations where you want to run a 250 tire, it allows the frame designer to bring the engine and tranny back to the centerline of the bike. I don't like shoving everything to the left to clear the tire, and upsetting the balance of the bike.

Why run a Twin Cam B motor and not A motor or an Evo?

Because it makes it easier to put the bike together. With the B motor there aren't any alignment issues or shimming of the transmission. No torque reaction between engine and transmission. No primary offset issues. Especially with the fat tire set up. There are still plenty of things you can do to make the motor fast. You can go to 116 cubes with aftermarket parts. It's a pretty simple choice, the Twin Cam B lowered the threshold of pain for assembling a scratch-built motorcycle. Everything just clicks together.

With the shim in place the rear of the struts is even with the front and both are positioned to keep the fender away from the tire.

The oil tank installs with the small brackets as shown. These allow plenty of adjustment so the tank can be installed as neatly as possible.

On the post-2000 soft-tail frames the seat post is no longer a major structural member and serves mostly as a place to mount the coil.

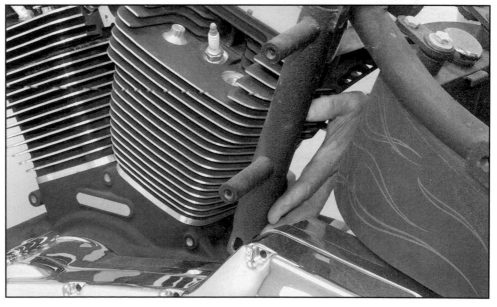

89

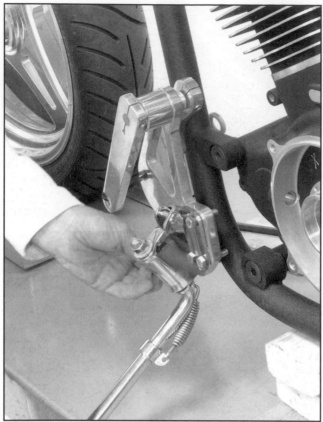

Installation of the forward controls comes next. Kick stand mounts off the left side control.

Attaching the right side control with the master cylinder requires partial disassembly.

Can anybody can buy one of these engines and transmissions from dealer?

Yes, just call the dealer or drive over, it's a regular part number. You can buy the engine in plain or black and chrome, it's a plug and play deal. Then buy the factory transmission case. All you need then is the Baker right side drive gearset kit. Obviously you will have to assemble the transmission or have someone assemble it for you.

What do you recommend for a wiring harness?

The easiest to use is the OEM H-D Softail harness. Pick one that matches the model and year of the engine you are using. You may have to hardwire a different plug for the aftermarket speedo, but that's as bad as it gets. Use the right factory coil, which is single fire. Plug in any aftermarket ignition module. With the factory harness it's easy to take it to the dealer for repairs or diagnostic work.

What's the hardest part of assembling this kit?

Deciding who, how and at what level. You can solve a lot of problems by having the pertinent shop manual to go with the drivetrain and frame configuration. So you have all the right specs and procedures.

What are the parts that aren't in the kit and why do you leave them out?

Foot pegs and hand grips because there are a million choices. Brakes for the same reason. Some people like full-floating rotors, some want a more typical polished rotor. Calipers, there are two, four and six piston models from all the different companies. The kit is setup with a solo seat, from there you are on your own. Taillight the same way, do you want a side mount or whatever.

90

Reassembly of the right side forward control starts with the lever assembly and the pushrod for the master cylinder.

With fender on bike, it's important to disconnect the shocks and bottom the suspension, then check the clearance between the fender/hardware and the tire.

A small Allen bolt and aluminum cap finish the reassembly and keep the pedal assembly in place on the pivot.

Design of Progressive shocks allows for ride height adjustment - though the point where bike bottoms is determined by the frame/swingarm, not the shocks.

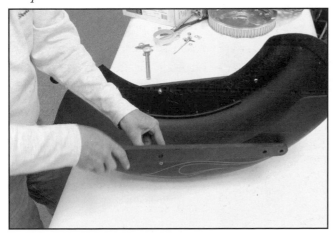

Before the struts are installed on the bike the fender is bolted to the strut.

To adjust the height, the big lock-nut is loosened and then the threaded collar can be screwed in or out of the shock body.

The inner primary is used only to contain the primary drive and not to absorb torque between engine and transmission.

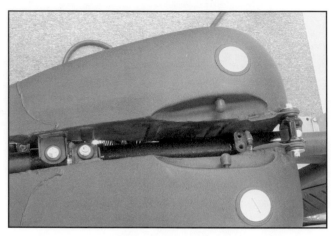

Fat bob tanks install in conventional fashion. Tank mounts are already installed on these frames.

The inner is a simple bolt on, without any spacers. Because this will be a display bike the actual primary drive will not be installed.

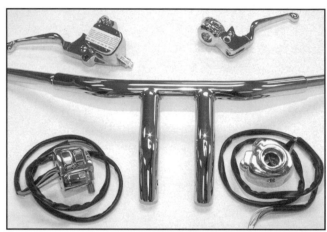

Skeeter recommends installing controls and switches before the bars are mounted on the bike. Controls and switches shown come with the kit.

The cover bolts on last. The RSD provision does not affect the inner primary and any normal chain or belt system designed for TC soft-tails can be used.

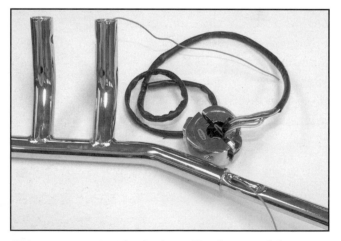

Wires are run inside the bars. You have to fish a small-gauge wire through first and use it to pull the harness through.

Can a person with only average mechanical abilities put one of these kits together?

When people ask me that at an event, I have a couple of qualifying questions for them:

Can you maintain a small block Chevy. That is, can you change oil and exhibit the logic needed to maintain a vehicle? Can you understand a repair manual? Second, why are you building the bike? If it's to have a cruiser, just go buy one. But if you want the accomplishment and the self esteem, of 'I did this myself,' then you are the person who should put one of these together. Because you do have to think and learn new things.

Do they need to do a full mock up?

Yes, I wouldn't build anything without a dry fitment. Bolt the bike together at least as far as you see it together in this sequence. You don't want to drill mounting holes in the dash or fender after they're painted. And you don't know that the delivery driver dropped the box and damaged the threads on an axle unless you screw the whole bike together.

How long to build a typical kit like this.

It's probably going to take 100 hours. You will put it together twice, as we mentioned. The quality of the end product is directly proportional to the amount of effort you put into the project. Murphy's law applies.

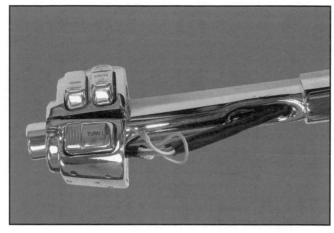

Skeeter pulls gently on the harness while pushing the switch into place, and waits to tighten the switch until the controls are correctly positioned.

Front fender mounts last, with bolts that come from the inside and through the spacer. Spacer and hardware come with the kit.

The Biker's Choice machine, as finished as it's going to get. With RSD and TC 88 B power, this is a thoroughly modern motorcycle that's relatively easy to assemble.

Chapter Six

Cory Ness Y2K Bike

A Ness-Designed Soft-Tail Alternative

The project seen here took place in the Arlen Ness shop in San Leandro, California. The bike being assembled is a chopper kit from the current Arlen Ness catalog. In this case we've also installed the optional engine and drivetrain, and a few other items not included in the kit. All in an effort to show the building of a complete motorcycle.

The kit comes with the chopper version of the Y2K 250 Dyna-style frame. Specifications

Cory Ness on the finished machine. A modern chopper with 250 rear tire, a rubber mounted engine and transmission for a smooth ride, and a very low seat height.

include 5 inches of backbone stretch and 4 inches of stretch in the front downtubes. The catalog lists a number of possible engines. The motor used in this project bike is a 113 inch S&S motor. The transmission is a five-speed assembled in the Ness shop using Zodiak gears and a one inch longer mainshaft.

The longer mainshaft is part of the way in which Arlen and Cory were able to design a frame that could accommodate a 250 rear tire with minimal engine and transmission offset.

Most of the wide tire frames currently on the market are soft-tail designs. Cory decided to build an alternative, a rubber-mount frame with room for a 250 or larger tire. By using a Dyna-style transmission case (which puts the oil tank under the transmission) and a sealed battery that can be laid on its side, Cory and his friends at the fabrication shop were able to design a rubber-mount frame with room for the largest tires and a scat height lower than that found on a typical soft-tail frame. Instead of welding together a series of straight tubing sections, this frame is made up of two loops of tubing that connect at the top tube and neck. The swingarm, fabricated from large diameter tubing, follows the

The "kit" assembled for this sequence is shown here. Not all the parts shown are included in a typical kit. Engine, transmission, primary drive, handlebar controls and wild paint are optional.

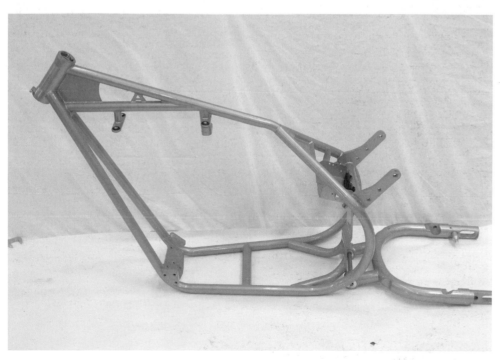

Where it all starts, with a bare Y2K 250 chassis. Note the way the frame is formed from two loops of large diameter tubing.

Ness Frame Manufacture

After being cut to length, the DOM seamless tubing is bent to the correct radius.

Manufacturing is done in two steps, step one is the manufacture of sub-assemblies like this one.

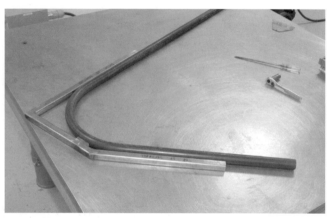

Making the new frame meant manufacturing a new bending die and determining the right sequence of bends. Each loop is checked after bending.

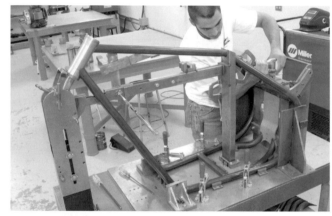

After machining the tubes where the neck and the other tubes meet the main sub-assembly (not shown), Rob puts everything back into the frame jig.

After bending, a left and right side loop are set into the very stout frame jig.

Everything is tack welded with the frame in the jig. Final welding is done with the frame standing free on the table to avoid building stress into the structure.

same large-radius design theme.

The bike built here has been assembled before, so the technician, Tim, knows that everything fits. He goes on to explain that, "People who buy these kits don't need to do a mock up. They should check the fit of the tanks and fenders, but we know the frames are straight and that all the major components will fit. The rear fenders come already drilled. The front fenders aren't drilled but they have a center-punch mark to show where they should be ventilated."

THE KIT

The kit is really a rolling chassis kit including the following: frame, rear shocks, fear fender struts, battery box side cover, front and rear fender, (available in steel or fiberglass), stretched gas tank, fork assembly with single disc, wheels, (a 18X8.50 inch rear and 18X3.00 or 21X2.15 inch front - both available in many styles), front and rear rotors, billet headlight, rear pulley, front and rear tires, transmission offset kit, forward controls foot pegs, handlebars with Allen bolts and dampener kit, front and rear caliper, axle spacers, motor mounts, fork bearings swingarm axle and bearings (a more complete description of the various parts is included in the Ness catalog).

Motor, transmission and primary drive are all assembled before installation into the frame. Rather than set the engine and transmission in the frame, the crew lays the engine and transmission on its side, then sets the frame down over the drivetrain.

The Dyna style drivetrain makes for easy installation of the engine and transmission. Here the front motor mount bolts are installed.

Once the motor mount bolts are installed, Tony and Tim flip the frame up onto the hoist.

The top motor mount link is adjusted to drop in without having to move the engine. Adjustment of this link will be checked later.

A bare frame with engine and transmission installed. Note the packing blanket on the hoist used to protect the paint.

Time to install the swingarm. Pivot bolt is coated with anti-seize. All bearings and bushings are from H-D and install per factory specifications.

Once the frame is right side up, Tim tightens and torques (22 to 28 ft. lbs.) the bolts that mount the engine to the front motor mount bracket.

Tim holds the swingarm in place and inserts the pivot bolt from the right.

As mentioned, this kit comes in various forms, each with its own sheet metal selection. Within each kit the buyer can make personal decisions as to fender and wheel selection. Kickstand, axle spacers, fork and swingarm bearings are included as well.

Hand controls, wiring harness, seat and a variety of small items are not included in the kit. Swingarm end caps are part of the kit though they come in a non-polished condition.

The Assembly Begins

The start of this assembly is a little different from the others seen in this book. Instead of lifting the engine into the frame, the 113 inch S&S engine and Dyna-style transmission, and complete chain-style primary, are set on the hoist as an assembly. Next, Tim and Tony drop the frame down over the assembled drivetrain.

Tim explains that he prefers to have the rear isolator (mount) bolted to the back of the transmission, and the front isolator and isolator -to-engine bracket bolted to the frame, before he drops the frame over the assembled engine and transmission.

Next he starts the bolts that attach the rear isolator to the frame, and the front bolts that attach the engine to the

As was done with the other kits in this book, all the threads on the Ness frame are cleaned out with a tap before any bolts are inserted.

Billet rear fender struts are a nice neat fit onto the small frame stubs. Before finalizing the fender installation Tim will check that the struts are parallel to each other.

At the Arlen Ness shop, wax is always used on the threads of chrome bolts whenever they are threaded into a chrome part or nut.

Lower shock mount is placed neatly inside the tubular swingarm. Large pin is locator for the brake caliper.

The two bolts that attach the struts to the frame are torqued to 30 ft. lbs.

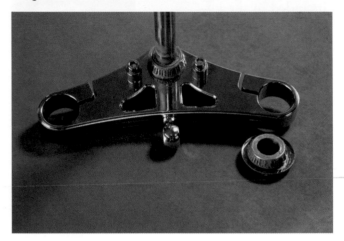

Ness trees and frame use the bolts and collars, as shown, for fork stops. Bearings are packed with boat-trailer (waterproof) wheel bearing grease.

Struts should be checked to ensure they are parallel and that they follow the centerline of the frame.

The lower tree and stem are pushed up from the bottom before the upper tapered bearing is dropped into place.

As shown in the photo, the billet aluminum fender struts must be parallel. "We use the thin brake shims, the ones that come with calipers, behind the strut to get them parallel," explains Tim. Once the swingarm and the shocks are in place Tim straps the frame in place on the hoist.

ASSEMBLE FORK

After packing the neck bearings with water proof wheel bearing grease the lower bearing is pressed

Initial adjustment of the neck bearings is done before the top tree and fork legs are in place. Tim sets it up a little on the tight side and then checks the adjustment once the fork and wheel are installed.

front isolator bracket. With the bolts for the front and rear mounts snug the frame is set right side up. The top mount with it's adjustable link is set "wherever it falls" after the front and rear mounts are tightened.

All the mounting bolts are tightened with a torque wrench. Tim keeps a Dyna service manual handy for looking up any torque specifications.

The policy in the Arlen Ness shop is to always use wax on chrome fasteners, "so they don't gall in the hole or nut," explains Tim. "The exception is critical bolts like rotor-to-hub bolts. In that case we run a tap into the hub to get rid of most of the chrome and then we put red Loctite on those, brake caliper bolts are treated the same way.

Installation of the swingarm comes next. Tim puts anti-seize on the through bolt and passes it through. The swingarm bushings used here are factory units. The through bolt is tightened to 45-50 ft. lbs.

Fork leg assemblies (tubes and lower legs) come already assembled and filled with oil. Here Tim slips the assembly up through the lower triple tree.

What holds the tubes in place is the nut on the top...

Handlebars are installed with two chrome Allen bolts. It's a good idea to clean the threads at the bottom of the bars before inserting the bolts.

...... and the pinch bolt in the lower triple tree.

Tony inserts the axle form the right side while Tim holds the front wheel in place.

A small metal strap, seen wrapped around the bushing in Tim's right hand, grounds the handle bars so the Whiskers lights will work.

This front end design uses an axle that screws directly into the left-side lower leg and is tightened to 50 ft. lbs.

102

down over the stem until it is seated on the lower triple tree (bearings, races and dust covers come with the kit but are not installed). These frames use an external fork stop so there is no lower collar to worry about. Before the top tree can be put in place Tim drops in the upper bearing, upper dust cap and the top nut. "I over-torque the bearings slightly," explains Tim, "so everything is seated, then I back off and adjust the top nut so there is no play. What feels a little too tight when you finish the adjustment will probably be about right after the tubes and wheel are in place. I do check it again according to the factory manual after everything is together, and you can get at the adjusting nut with a slim punch under the tree if you need to change the adjustment." The top tree is attached after the nut is adjusted, and held in place with a single chrome bolt.

The fork tubes come as an assembly and installation is pretty straightforward, just slip the tube up through the lower tree (with a little WD-40 on the tubes), put the nut on the top, and then tighten the lower pinch bolt, "so the tube doesn't turn," then tighten the top nut to 11 to 22 ft. lbs., then loosen the lower pinch bolt and re-tighten it to ensure that the

There are two pinch bolts in the bottom of the right-side lower leg that lock the axle in place, and a chrome cap to keep it all neat.

Before installing the billet rear wheel the 70 tooth, 1-1/8 inch Tri-star pulley and brake rotor are installed.

103

With the shocks installed, Jeff holds the wheel up while Tim slips the axle into place.

Caliper carrier is in essence anther axle spacer and must be installed with the wheel. Caliper lock pin is installed with Loctite.

Getting the axle and spacers in place while holding up the wheel definitely requires at least four hands. Axle spacers are included with the kit.

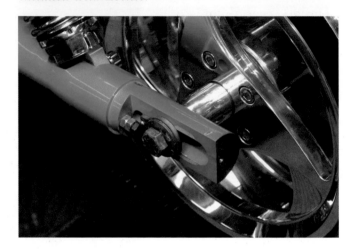

Belt tension is adjusted with the adjusters as shown.

Left side shot shows the flush mount axle and the spacer used between the frame and the pulley.

Once wheel is in place and belt position is correct the second nut on the adjuster can be jammed against the first.

tube is correctly seated in both trees.

Many of the Arlen Ness bikes use the small "whiskers" turn signals bolted into the stem for the turn signal. These lights ground to the bars, which means there must be some provision to ground the bars themselves. This is taken care of when Tim puts the handlebar bushings in place, with a little ground strap. Before he actually screws the bars in place Tim performs one extra step. "We always run the tap up into the threads on the bottom of the bars, to clean out the chrome and the weld slag."

After the rotor is bolted to the front wheel hub and the bolts tightened, the wheel itself is set up into place between the fork legs. The axle comes in from the right fork leg, any spacers needed to center the wheel between the fork legs are included with the kit. Tony tightens the front axle to 50 ft. lbs. then tightens the two pinch bolts that come up from the bottom, and finally installs the small chrome cap.

REAR WHEEL AND BELT ADJUSTMENT.

After the pulley and rotor are installed on the rear wheel hub, Jeff and Tim install the rear wheel and axle. Again, the spacers

The true test of wheel position and belt tension is made by spinning the wheel in a forward direction and then checking to see how the belt tracks in the pulley.

Once Tim is happy with the belt tension and the way it runs on the pulley he tightens both axle bolts to 60 ft. lbs.

After the spin-test the belt should not be crowded up against either side of the pulley.

A progress shot. Wheels and drivetrain installed, now it's time for sheet metal and wiring.

come with the kit. Note the assembly sequence shown in the photos. The lock pin needed for the rear caliper carrier is installed on the right side with Loctite.

First, Tim gets the wheel position close and the belt tension about right, based on the position of the axle in the swingarm. Then he uses the adjusters to fine tune the wheel position, "you want the belt to crowd to the outside just a little bit," says Tim, "when the wheel is spinning in a forward direction." When the spacers are correct you need not worry about the axle position, it should fall into place. The final tightening of the axle nuts is done with the torque wrench to a reading of 60 ft. lbs.

FORWARD CONTROLS

With the rear wheel in place Tim swings the bike on the hoist and pinches the front wheel in the vise. Installing the forward controls comes next, the actual installation requires more than just bolting the assembly onto the bike. The master cylinder seen in the sequence is a Radius master cylinder. The sexy design comes at a price: the master cylinder must be removed from the rest of the assembly in order to bolt the whole thing onto the bike. It's not too complicated but could be a little confusing.

Rather than try to explain each step we're provided a sequence of photos that show why and how the right side forward control is disassembled, bolted to the bike and reassembled.

Once the master cylinder is in place it's important to check the free play adjustment before putting the master cylinder into service. The instructions (that come with the kit)

The right side forward control must be disassembled prior to installation.

.... and then the master cylinder.

Tim starts by removing the lever.....

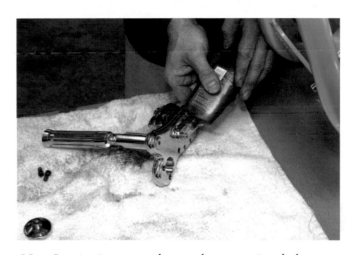

Now Loctite is squeezed onto the mounting bolts.....

.....followed by the thin wave spring......

.... and the forward control can now be mounted on the frame.

Ness Complete V-twin Program

Engines from Arlen and Cory can be powder coated to match your frame. You can even specify polished fins with powder coated cylinders and heads as shown.

At the Ness facility, you can buy nearly any aftermarket engine you can dream up. From basic 100 cubic inch engines in black and silver to complete 124 cubic inch brutes with polished cases and powder coated cylinders.

Possible bore sizes include both 4, 4-1/8 and 4-1/4 inches, while strokes run from 4 to 4-5/8 inches. Though they build a large number of engines based on S&S components, Merch and Patrick Racing components are also listed.

Polishing and diamond cutting are both readily available. If it's color you need to match or compliment the paint on the bike, powder coating is available in a rainbow of colors. What makes it relatively easy for Arlen and Cory to provide such a wide array of possible finishes is the fact that all the polishing and powder coating are done in-house.

The engine of your choice can be shipped to you assembled or in pieces. All complete engines are test run prior to shipping, so you know the new mill will fire right up once you have them installed in the frame (minor jet changes may be required after installation).

Aesthetic options include the full gamut of billet and chrome covers and accessories seen in the Ness catalog. Order yours in simple S&S trim, or with a complete billet radius package from Arlen and Cory.

If you're wondering what your dream engine might cost, just contact Arlen's. They can fax you a "menu," and will have a quote ready shortly after you fax the form back to their office.

At the house of Ness, you can buy your V-twin in nearly any size imaginable, assembled or in kit form as shown. Kits are complete right down to the chrome fasteners.

Of Longer Mainshafts

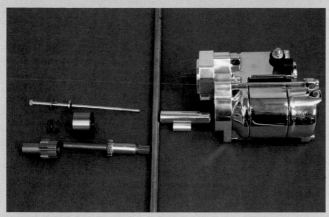

Starter blow up, vertical bar represents inner primary. Note starter with extended coupler. Parts on left make up the drive assembly.

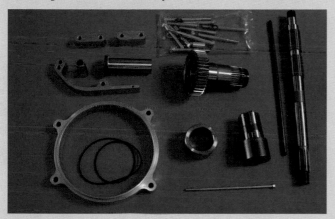

This offset kit sold by Arlen's can be used to move the drive belt over on both Dyna and post-2000 Softails.

Complete, polished, 5-speed transmissions can be purchased with the longer mainshaft already installed.

Stuffing a 250 rear tire in a Dyna-style frame, with belt drive, requires certain provisions to move the belt over far enough to clear the tire. In the case of many pre-2000 soft-tail chassis, the entire transmission was moved over in the chassis which in turn would move the belt over far enough to clear the wide tires. This strategy is possible because the engine and transmission are bolted to the frame as separate units.

The trouble with the Dyna-style drivetrain is the essentially unitized engine and transmission. You can't just slide the tranny over because it's bolted to the back of the engine. The way out of this dilemma is to manufacture a longer mainshaft for the transmission. In this way the drive pulley, and the final drive belt, are moved over far enough so the belt clears the rear tire. It's never quite that simple of course. Because now the entire primary drive has been moved over one inch, which requires the use of a spacer between the engine and inner primary, and an adapter to move the compensator sprocket over as well. Even the starter needs a spacer and longer through-bolt so the drive will reach the relocated clutch basket with the teeth on the outer rim.

The official Ness kit for adding a 250 tire to Dyna and post-2000 soft-tail chassis includes all the items mentioned above. The offset kit is included with the Ness Builder's kits though you will need a five-speed transmission to modify. To make things simpler, the crew at the Ness facility also sell complete five-speed transmissions with the longer mainshaft kit already installed. You can even buy that complete transmission with the case already polished to a bright shine.

The rest of the installation is pretty straight forward. Here Tim installs another mounting bolt.

Reinstalling the lever and chrome cap finishes the installation of the right side forward control.

The master cylinder is reinstalled next, you have to be sure the pushrod engages the piston.

A banjo bolt is used to attach the line to the bottom of the master cylinder. The brake lines do not come with the kit.

This Allen bolt comes in from the back side - a good spot for a ball-end Allen wrench.

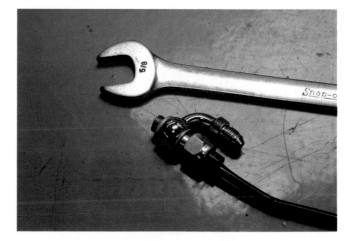

This clever brake light switch is used at the rear brake caliper.

explain how to adjust the free play to 1/16 inch if the free play is not correct.

The left side forward control is a simple bolt-on proposition and will be installed a little later.

Now it's time to install the rear brake line. Of note, the line does not come with the kit. Tim installs the line at the master cylinder with a banjo bolt and two new sealing washers, then routes the line along the frame and back to the area where the rear caliper will be bolted on. To keep it neatly out of the way Tim clamps the hose to the frame with frame clamps or tie wraps.

The bracket for the rear caliper was installed when the rear wheel was set up into place. Now the caliper is bolted to the bracket. Red Loctite is used on the two caliper-mounting bolts. As we've said before, it's important to center the caliper over the rotor with the thin shims, and it's likewise important to use the caliper mounting bolts that come with the kit.

Instead of using a standard banjo bolt, Tim uses a special bolt with an integral brake light switch, to attach the brake line to the rear caliper. This makes for a very neat installation. As

The finished and installed master cylinder complete with a braided steel brake line.

As mentioned elsewhere, the caliper must be centered over the rotor. The caliper does come with the kit, also included are a series of shims that can be used to move the caliper to the outside.

The final bleeding is done in a conventional way, by building pressure in the master cylinder and then opening the bleeder screw. By running the hose from the bleeder into a container filled with brake fluid it's easier to see the bubbles when the bleeder is opened. After bleeding Tim checks for leaks.

Installing the left side forward control is pretty simple with none of the extra steps needed for the other side.

Tim describes it, "I hide the line behind the swingarm and the wires behind the line."

BLEEDING

Tim likes to use what is essentially an EZ Bleeder. This over-sized syringe pushes the brake fluid in from the bleeder until the master cylinder reservoir is filled. "As you push the fluid in from the open bleeder, the first thing you see is bubbles in the master cylinder," explains Tim. "Then when the bubbles are gone and just fluid comes up into the master, you're basically done. You still have to pump it a few times to get a good pedal, and then I bleed it in the conventional way, with the bleeder, with a clear hose in place on the bleeder. On the first opening of the bleeder you generally get a little squirt of air, I pump the pedal, open the bleeder (while holding the pedal down) and look for air three times, that's plenty for most of these.

INSTALL THE HANDLEBAR AND CONTROLS

Like the other sequences seen in this book, the wires from the handlebar controls are run inside the handle bars. The Ness controls used on this bike (which do not come with the kit) include small button switches for the starter and the right side

Once the left side forward control is installed, the shift rod can be put in place and adjusted.

The brake lines use separate ends like the 30 degree banjo end seen here.

The single front caliper is next on the install list.

The brake line itself routes from the caliper to the master cylinder through the bracket seen here on the bottom of the lower tree.

Like the rear, the caliper kit ships with shims that Tim used to center the caliper over the rotor.

The throttle assembly contains a ball bearing which seats on the bolt head seen under Tim's thumb.

The billet headlight housing is included in the kit and bolts to the lower tree. The necessary headlight bulb is not included.

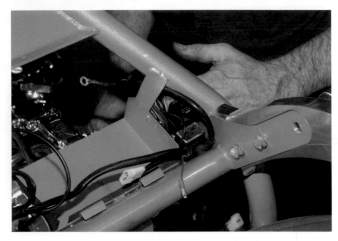

The wiring module is mounted to the right of the battery box. Small size makes it easy to mount the module in a snug spot like this.

Foam sheets are cut to size and used to line the battery box.

blinker. The Ness bars have a divider inside the main bar so it's easier to fish wires through the bars. Prior to pulling the wires from the switch through the bars Tim fishes an old throttle cable through the bars, tapes the wires to the cable and gently pulls them through.

Lights are part of the switch assembly, the turn signal switch is in series with the light. On the left side, for example, there is only one wire, it runs to power. Depress the switch, close the circuit, the other "wire" not visible, goes to ground.

The throttle assembly (again, not part of the kit) uses a roller bearing at the outside of the handle bar to support the throttle and make for smooth operation. Before the throttle is assembled on the bike Tim installs the support for the bearing on the end of the bar. The throttle is a single cable "pull" system (you can order the throttle assembly with either a single or dual cable), and Tim puts the throttle grip assembly on the bar end and routes the cable over to the carburetor. Once the cable is in place and routed correctly the adjuster is used to take the slack out of the cable.

WIRING

In the Arlen Ness shop they use the Wiring Plus harness kit (not part of the chassis kit). The first step in the job of wiring the bike is to set the small module in place on the right side of the battery box (note the photos). The flasher for the turn signals is placed on the other side of the battery box. Before installing the battery, protective pads are glued on the inside of the box. These will cushion the battery from vibration, and protect it from the small machine screws and nuts on the right side that attach the fuse box to the battery box. Now the battery and then the battery strap can be installed.

"One of my pet peeves is sloppy wiring," explains Tim. "I like to take my time and make it really neat." Tim's knack for neatness includes the installation of the small flexible wire between the frame and the engine, at the rear mount. This is to ensure the frame is properly

Cory used a number of tricks - like using a sealed battery mounted on its side - to keep the seat height low.

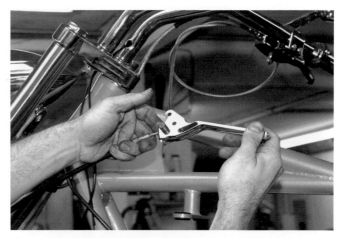

Tim routes the cable for the clutch and attaches it to the handle bar control.

Battery is held in with a strap. Ignition switch will mount to the wrap around side cover or "oil tank."

This adjusting sleeve is used to take most of the play out of the clutch cable. By making the sleeve assembly longer, clutch lever free play is reduced.

Lower angle shows the flasher for the turn signals and the hot wire that runs from the regulator to the battery or main relay.

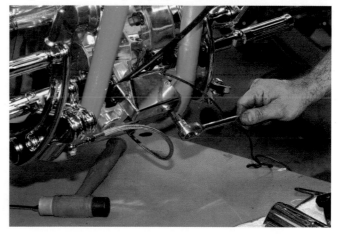

Billet regulator attaches to bracket that is bolted to the frame as shown. It's important that there be a good ground between frame and regulator base.

Per the instructions that come with the engine, the dual-fire coil is connected to the Crane HI 4 ignition.

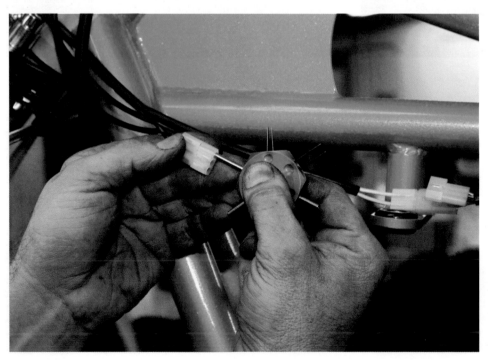

Each wire connector is held into the plastic terminal block with a small tang. If you make a mistake and have to get a connector out of the terminal block you need a tool like the one in Tim's right hand.

grounded. The regulator is installed on its own bracket. Of the three wires that exit the regulator two go to the Stator plug and one runs to the battery or main relay. Because the relay isn't very accessible, Tim runs the hot wire from the regulator to the positive battery terminal.

There are a total of three wire connections on the positive battery terminal: the battery cable, the hot wire to regulator and the power wire to the circuit board.

Most of the wiring follows the instructions that come with the Wiring Plus kit. There are a few notes however: Tim does use a VOES switch, which he tucks in behind the battery. The wire from the HI 4 ignition module (green) goes to a wire from VOES switch (with a pink connector). Two wires go to coil, power and trigger, both come from the module.

There are two small, three-wire plugs that run to the front of the bike, one is headlight wires. The other runs to the handlebar control buttons. Near the end of the wiring sequence, Tim installs the license plate light and swingarm end cap. These end caps do not come polished. The three-wire plug seen in the photos had to be installed.

The clutch cable was installed mid-way through the wiring job. The engine and transmission were

If you need more connectors, most shops have a selection of terminal blocks and terminals like those seen here.

At Arlen and Cory's shop they like to use a single-pull throttle, though you can order a complete engine package with either single or double-pull cables.

You can see the VOES switch mounted on the left of the battery. Because this is a rubber-mount engine, there needs to be a ground from engine to frame.

Threaded collar seen here is used to take the slack out of the throttle cable. Wire for blinker comes down through the center of the stud.

Side-mount license bracket and taillight are designed to mount to the end of the swingarm These do not come with the kit.

Here you can see the neat routing of the throttle cable before the gas tank goes on.

Engines from the Ness shop are pre-run - the oil pump is already primed. Tim starts with 2 quarts, runs the engine and then checks the oil.

Primary lube should come up to the bottom of the diaphragm spring as shown with the bike level.

Instead of a dip stick, this transmission uses a small weep hole. Note the lube running out of the hole.

already assembled, with the clutch cable attached, so Tim only had to attach the cable at the lever and route it neatly. Then the adjusting sleeve is used to take most of the slack out of the cable. After the adjustment, Tim left 3/32 inch of play (factory spec) between the ferule on the cable and the control housing. This is more accurate then measuring the play at the lever.

At this point the new green Y2K chopper is starting to look like a motorcycle. There is no lubricant in the engine, transmission or primary, and the next job is to fill all three. The oil tank for the engine is filled with two quarts of oil. According to Tim, "that's enough to get the oil circulating and the oil filter filled. Then after we shut it off I will check it again."

The tranny is filled next. There is no dip stick here, the billet cover uses a weep hole instead, note the photo. The primary case is filled through the derby cover and filled to the bottom edge of the clutch diaphragm spring.

SHEET METAL AND FUEL LINE

The frame kit comes with a stretched steel tank and tank mounts welded to the frame. Installing the tank is nothing more than screwing in the petcock and running the bolts up through the frame mounts (with a rubber insert in each mounting point) into the bungs welded into the bottom of the steel tank.

Installation of the battery cover requires drilling three small holes in the cover. In the Ness shop they mount the ignition switch and the high-low switch in the left side-cover. Next, Tim runs a fuel line from the petcock to the filter, and from the filter to the carburetor. Crimp clamps are used instead of the more common screw variety, "because they're neater," (they also require the use of a special pliers for a neat crimp) and a stainless cover is cut and slid over the gas line before installation.

The front and rear fenders go in place pretty easily. In both cases the boys like to use a hardened washer on either side of the fender, "so the fender doesn't get chewed up, especially with the fiberglass fenders."

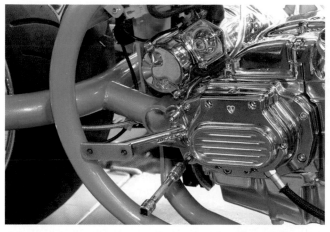

Now we're getting somewhere. Bracket for exhaust bolts to the back of the transmission.

Gas lines (5/16 inch) are cut to length and shielded with stainless wrap.

Ignition switch mounts to the side cover (after drilling a hole) with the help of a special wrench.

Tim likes the crimp clamps "because they're so neat." They do, however, require the use of a special pliers.

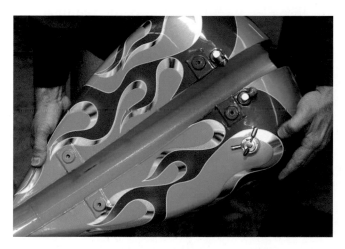

Gas tanks come with mounts already welded in to the bottom.

With help from Dustin, Tim installs the front fender.

Rear fender is installed with care. Note the shop rags hanging on the fender struts. The fit of the fender and struts was checked during the mock-up phase.

Hardened washers are used on both sides of the fender, this is done on the front fender as well. Washers prevent rails from digging into the paint when the bolts are tightened.

Before mounting the rear fender Tim drops the shocks and cranks the bike up high to make it easier to mount the fender. Even on the rear fender Tim uses a hardened washer on either side of the fender, note the photo. "Otherwise you end up with a crease all the way around the fender right where it hits the strut. With the fender in place Tim cranks the bike back down and re-attaches the bolts for the shocks.

EXHAUST

The support bracket must be installed onto the back of the transmission before the pipes go on. Like some other technicians seen in this book, Tim uses the small exhaust gaskets. The rear pipe is attached loosely first, and the bolts snugged up on the mount. Next comes the front pipe, installed following the same procedure. You have to be sure the pipes fit and are positioned correctly before you do the final tightening of the flange nuts. Then the bracket bolts can be tightened for the last time.

FINAL ADJUSTMENTS AND CHECKS

Before sending the bike down the road Tim likes to swing the bike so the front fork is hanging free, then check the adjustment of the neck bearings. "The pinch bolts in the lower trees must be tight," explains Tim. "So that if you get a little slop when you pull on the fork you know it's in the neck bearings and not the tubes or where the tubes meet the tree. There shouldn't be any play in the bearings. The top tapered bolt, in the center of the top tree, locks down the adjusting nut, and adds to the load on the nut. So to check the final adjustment you have to have the taper-head bolt in place."

Tim adds that the fork should "fall" to the side as described in the factory service manual. If it doesn't, the neck adjusting nut can be adjusted (without removing the top tree) with a very thin screwdriver or a thin piece of metal used like a punch.

The fork stop can be adjusted with shims under the small BHCS bolts on either side. With these handle bars the fork can be allowed to turn fairly sharp. Be sure to leave at least the width of a finger between the bars and the tank

Here you can see how the use of the washers keeps the fender from being sucked up against the inside of the strut.

Time to mount the Arlen Ness exhaust pipes. Tim hangs each pipe, and makes sure the flanges are correctly seated before he starts to tighten everything up.

Angle gauge place on the front rotor should have the same reading as one placed on the rear rotor.

Flange nuts should be fully tightened before you do the final tightening of the bracket bolts.

Before calling it done, Tim swings the bike around on the hoist and checks the adjustment of the neck bearings with the wheel and fork hanging free.

Like Kendall in the first sequence, Tim starts the bleeding sequence by "bubbling" the master cylinder.

at their closest point. A low speed tumble in the parking lot often moves the fork a little past the normal stopping point. You don't want a little mishap like that to put a big dent in the tank.

Before taking the bike off the hoist, with the wheel center lines lined up, Tim puts a angle gauge on the rear rotor and checks that against the front rotor. If the two don't agree the upper engine link needs to be fine adjusted (remember, the swingarm is mounted to the rear of the transmission housing).

To bleed the front brakes. Tim used the big syringe again to push fluid in from the bleeder. Once the reservoir is full he bleeds it in the conventional fashion with the bleeder at the caliper. Note the clear tubing that runs the fluid to the container. This way you can see the bubbles in the fluid.

START UP AND ROAD TEST

It's a good idea to put an oil gauge on the engine when the bike is first started. All complete engines shipped from Arlen's are pre-run, so the oil pump is primed but you do want to be sure the engine has good oil pressure before running it for very long. Tim follows recommendations in a recent service manual from S&S for initial start-up: One minute at 1250 to 1750 RPM. No revving or load, check for oil

Once no more bubble are visible in the master, Tim bleeds the front caliper in the conventional fashion, as was done with the rear caliper.

122

leaks and oil pressure. After allowing engine to cool he starts it again and allows it to warm up a short time (less than four minutes) before shutting it off again.. The start-and-cool cycle should be repeated three or four times, allowing the engine to get slightly warmer each time. RPM can be varied gently from idle to 2500, the engine should not be allowed to get too hot during these cycles. Now the normal break-in procedure can start.

The first road test should be a short one. Take it easy with the brakes on the first few stops. Once you've got the bike back in the shop take some time to look for any obvious trouble spots. Is the belt rubbing on the tire, is anything obviously loose?

After the first hundred miles it's a good idea to take the wrenches and check all the nuts and bolts on the bike. The first oil change should come at 50 miles, another at 500, then 2500 and every 2500 after that. At 500 miles you need to check the tension of the final drive belt and the primary chain.

Left side of the finished machine. "Loop" frame helps to give the bike nice lines. Raised neck used with this particular frame provides for a bit of that chopper silhouette.

The Y2K 250 bikes are available in various configuration, not just the chopper seen here. With a low seat height, smooth ride and 250 tire they represent a good alternative to a soft-tail bike.

Chapter Seven

American Thunder Chopper

A Blend of Old and New with RSD

The project shown here is the assembly of a 250mm Chopper kit from American Thunder in Prior Lake, Minnesota just south of Minneapolis. As this is the fourth assembly in the book, we've tried to go light on certain parts

of the assembly that have been covered in the other sequences, and heavy on topics that we might not have covered adequately in the other three bike-building series.

If what you want to build is a chopper, here's your chance. The 250 Chopper kit from American Thunder utilizes a Rolling Thunder frame with raised neck and long springer fork. Like many rolling chassis kits, this one can be purchased with or without the drivetrain.

The Kit

The kit from American Thunder uses a Rolling Thunder chopper-style frame with soft-tail rear suspension, set up to run right side drive. If the neck looks a little tall, it's because the downtubes are stretched six inches while the backbone is stretched two inches.

This rolling chassis kit comes with the frame including swingarm, pivot shaft and bolts, a one inch rear axle and the half inch primary spacer. Also included are the swingarm bushings, shocks, handle bars with mounting hardware, "14 over" Rolling Thunder springer with necessary hardware including upper and lower neck bearings, forward controls, one piece gas tank, front and rear fender, 21 inch front and 18 inch rear wheels, Avon tires, along with some bolts and hardware. To round out this kit, Neil has added a 124 inch S&S engine, six-speed Baker RSD transmission, primary drive and all the hardware needed to make it a running motorcycle.

When we come in, the frame is already powder painted in an electric yellow by Best Coat, from Blaine, Minnesota. T. J. Design,

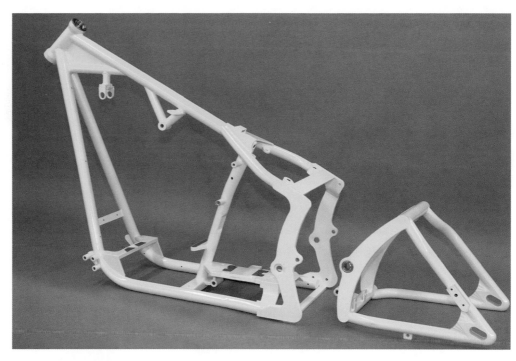

Before sending the soft-tail frame out for powder coating, Neal and Troy did a full mock-up, including the addition of some brackets that can't be fabricated once the paint is applied.

Troy likes to test fit the cross shaft and align the pivot bolts before the swingarm is actually installed.

Troy recommends using anti-seize on the big pivot bolts. There is a washer used between the frame and swingarm on either side.

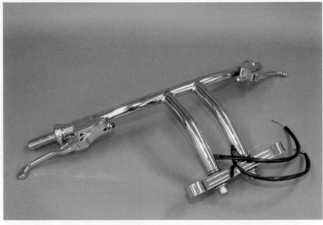

It's easier to assemble controls before the bars go on the bike. Controls are from PM, 11/16 inch clutch master works best with the Baker hydraulic clutch.

Installing the springer fork is a two person operation, Neal holds the fork while Troy installs the top bearing and nut.

Here you can see the three Allen bolts that hold the upper triple tree in place.

A special spanner wrench is used to adjust the neck bearings. Troy adjusts the bearings based on experience, but will check the adjustment again once the upper tree and wheel are in place.

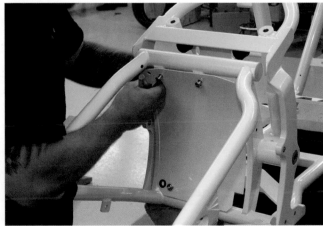

The rock shield was painted along with the rest of the frame and should be installed once the swingarm is in place.

126

another local firm, matched the liquid paint used on the sheet metal to the color of the frame.

THE ASSEMBLY BEGINS

As with all the other projects, Troy Lutgen, technician at American Thunder, starts by cleaning all the threads, the areas where the bearing races install in the neck, and the very top of the neck where the dust shield seats.

After installing the swingarm pivot bearings, Troy installs the swingarm, with the comment that, "if this were a belt-drive bike the belt would go on now, before the swingarm is bolted in place."

Next, the rubber snubbers are installed on the frame followed by the rock shield. Of note, there are some additional brackets on this frame, added during the mock-up stage, for the exhaust bracket and the air suspension. Also, the forward controls sit farther forward because the owner of this bike is well over six feet tall.

Installation of the fork is next. After

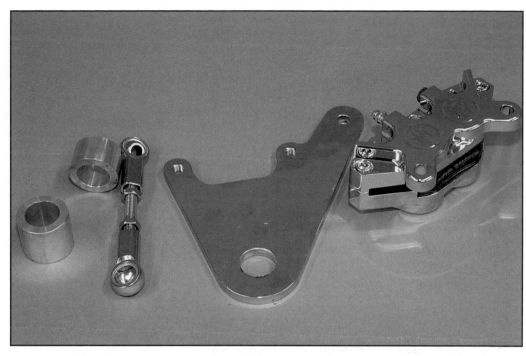

Rear brake doesn't automatically come with the rolling chassis kit. Caliper and bracket used here are from PM. American Thunder ships the wheel spacers with the kit only if you order the brakes when you order everything else.

Installing the rear wheel is just a matter of rolling it into place and installing the correct spacers - determined earlier.

Installing the front wheel is a two-person operation. Spacers (which do not come with the kit) center the wheel in the fork.

With a little help from Ken, Troy drops the big S&S motor in place.

Axle sits flush in the fork, held in place by a big chrome Allen on either side. Note the torque wrench.

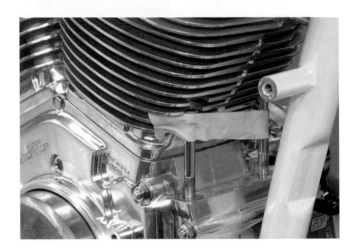

The back motor mount bolts are set into the case, and taped up as shown, before the engine is dropped onto the frame.

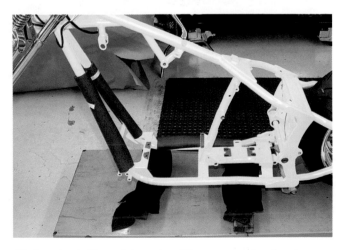

Before installing the engine Troy wraps the frame tubes with protective insulation. Note the bare-metal mounting points.

Installation of the six-speed transmission is next.

packing the bearings Neil holds the fork in place while Troy installs the upper bearing and adjusting nut. Like some other modern fork and triple tree assemblies, this one has no real provision for adjusting the neck bearings once the top tree is in place. Troy tightens the nut a little too tight to start with, backs off slightly, and then does the final adjustment by feel. The handle bars are added at this time, along with the upper triple tree. Note that the controls and wires are already mounted and run before the bars are set onto the bike. The bolts that hold the top tree to the fork are coated with Loctite and tightened to 35 to 40 ft. lbs.

At this point Neil and Troy install the rear wheel. Troy explains that "we do supply the spacers for the rear wheel when the customer buys the brakes from us." Rather than install the rear shocks at this time Troy puts a solid bar in place between the frame and the swingarm. The shocks will be installed later after the transmission is in place.

The front wheel is next. These come with sealed bearings so there is no need to set up the wheel and check the end play. Troy slides the axle in place from the left side. The springer-style caliper bracket uses a wave spring that must be included so the caliper can pivot without being too loose. The axle tightens up with an Allen bolt that comes in from either side. "I like to use red Loctite on those Allen bolts," explains Troy. "There aren't any lock washers so it seems like a good idea." The Allens are tightened to 55 ft. lbs.

The front caliper is installed and centered over the rotor. "I use red Loctite on the bolts that hold the caliper to the bracket," says Troy, "but I put wax on chrome bolts that go into the Nylock nuts."

Most RSD frames are designed to use a 1/2 inch primary spacer, as shown.

Before the inner primary goes on you need to be sure the inner bearing race is in place on the shaft (as shown) and that the shift lever is in place.

Sometimes holes in the inner primary that slip over dowels are a little too small, due to a build up of chrome, and must be opened up with a drill. Troy runs a tap into threaded holes for the same reason.

The Clutch

In pieces a '90-'93 clutch, on the right a '98 and later clutch assembly, note the difference in the teeth (finer teeth were used starting in '94)...

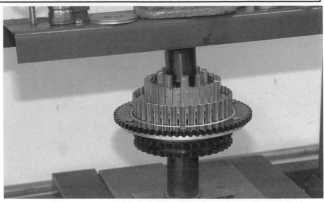

Then the action moves to the press where the clutch hub (the inner part).....

...bigger teeth are less likely to strip when used on big engines. Starter gear must match ring gear.

...is pressed into the clutch shell (the outer section with the ring gear).

Assembling a clutch starts with the positioning of this tool as shown.

Discs come in metal and fiber and must be inserted in alternating sequence per the manual.

The Clutch

"Sharp edge" on metal discs should go down. Discs must slide in easily, there is a heavy spring plate installed in the middle of the pack.

Pressure plate and diaphragm spring go on after all discs are in place.

Fiber discs should be soaked in primary fluid before assembly. Pack starts and ends with fiber.

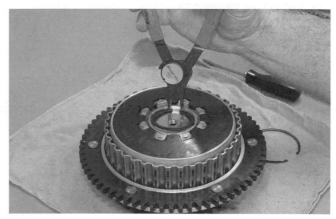

Next the release plate is installed and locked in place with the snap ring.

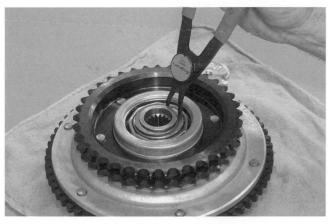

Clutch hub retaining snap ring goes on the back side.

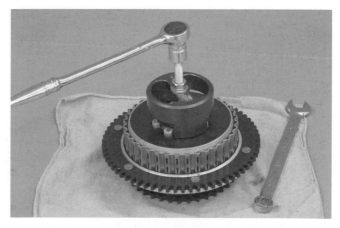

Now the spring is compressed with the special tool and held in place with a retaining ring.

With the engine tight and the inner primary snug, Troy tries hardened washers under the transmission mounts as shown.

Regulator must have a good ground, note the star-washers used between the regulator and the bracket.

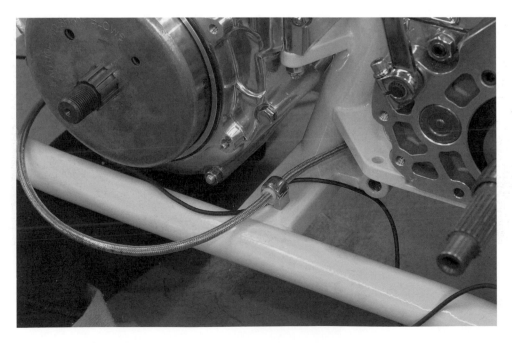

DRIVETRAIN

The engine is installed next, after protective tubing is wrapped around the frame tubes. Troy sets the transmission onto the frame, without any nuts on the studs, followed by the spacer for the primary and then the inner primary. The inner primary is from CCI and comes unassembled as was detailed in the Goliath kit sequence.

"After tightening down the engine bolts to 35 ft. lbs. and snugging up the inner primary, I look at the points where the transmission sits on the mounts," explains Troy. "If there's any space there I use a hardened brake spacer (the ones that come with the calipers) between the tranny and the mount. I just try to slide a series of washers into place until I find one that fits snug" (note the photo).

After determining which shim goes where, Troy takes off the inner primary, lifts the tranny up, installs the spacer, sets it back down and tightens the Nylock nuts to 35 ft.lbs. on each stud. Now the inner primary is re-installed, but not for the last time. Troy's fitting sequence isn't quite finished, as he explains. "After I've got the transmission tightened down, then I pull the inner primary off again to see if it slides off and on easily. Then it can go on for the last time,

Before the inner primary is installed for the last time, the small bracket from Chimaera is bolted to the frame (the hole in the frame was drilled and tapped during the mock up). The hose is the hydraulic line to the clutch, the wire is the hot wire from regulator to the battery.

Note how the little lock tabs have been bent over the heads of the inner primary bolts.

...Troy does this four separate times, moving the shaft 90 degrees each time. If it doesn't snap back it means the drive will hang up later.

With a coating of oil on all the parts the starter drive assembly is bolted in place.

The primary drive must be installed as an assembly, though the clutch isn't completely assembled yet.

Once the long jack shaft bolt is tightened it's important to pull the starter drive out against the spring and see that it snaps back into place....

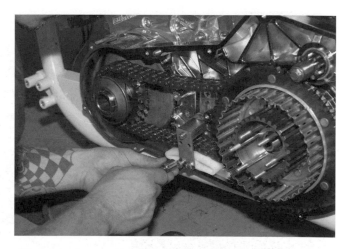

Now it's time to install the "foot" and adjust the chain tension.

The clutch hub nut is left hand thread. Pushrod for clutch slides up inside the hole in the transmission shaft.

complete with the lock tabs on the inner primary bolts, which are tightened to 22 ft. lbs." Troy warns that the fifth transmission stud might have to be shortened slightly if it's too close to the shocks.

Though this could be done later, the regulator is mounted now, after a little paint is sanded off the frame to ensure a good ground. Next the 1.6 Kw Terry Components starter is installed per the sequences shown elsewhere in the book.

The primary used here is a chain style, with a heavy duty Bandit clutch assembly. Before setting the whole thing up and into the inner primary, Troy slides the pushrod up inside the transmission shaft. As was mentioned before, the clutch-hub nut is left hand thread, and should be tightened to 80 ft. lbs. While the 1-1/2 inch nut for the compensator sprocket is tightened to 160 ft. lbs. The "foot" is installed just under the lower run of primary chain. Before setting the initial tension for the chain, Troy checks the runout for the primary chain only to find the forward end is a full .080 inch closer in than the clutch end. Resolving this means removal of the

Troy explains that the foot for the primary chain mounts as shown, "lots of people put this in wrong."

entire assembly, and the installation of a .080 inch shim under the compensator sprocket. Troy feels that if you have to be off a little on the alignment, it's better to have the compensator end of the primary chain farther out, rather than closer in.

With a 124 cubic inch engine and a rider who intends to fully utilize all that power, the decision was made early on to use a 530 chain for the final drive. The actual chain that Troy used was a little too long, which meant shortening it by two links. Most chains now use press-fit connecting links in place of the old master links, and these are most easily installed with a special tool (not shown).

WIRING AND SHEET METAL

At this point we took a little break in the assembly. When the action picks up again, Troy has the bike pretty much ready for wiring and sheet metal.

American Thunder is in the midst of building their own wiring kit. In designing the kit Neil tried to use all water-proof connectors, much like Harley-Davidson and most OEM automotive companies are doing. On this particular bike the owner wanted the wires run up inside the frame, which meant the bundles of wiring had to be run through the frame before the ends could be pushed into the terminal blocks. When a more typical kit buyer installs one of these kits however, most of the terminal blocks will be in place and he or she will be able to simply install the main module behind the battery, route the wires and plug A into B. The exception will be the handlebar wiring. Builders will still have to run the wires through the bars and then attach the terminal blocks to the bundle emerging from each side of the handle bars, so the handle bar harnesses can be plugged into the main harness.

Among the other things that need to be done here, near the end of the project, is routing and connecting brake lines. Up front the

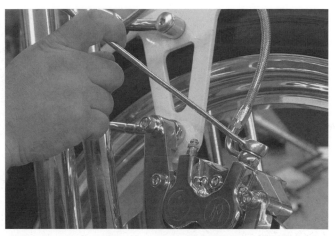

Troy tightens up the banjo bolt for the front caliper - with two new sealing washers in place. All connections like this should be checked later for leaks.

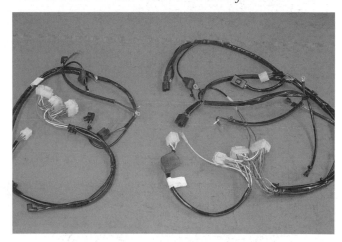

Wiring options: On the left a factory Softail harness for 1989. On the right a 1993 harness with plug-in for the self-cancelling module.

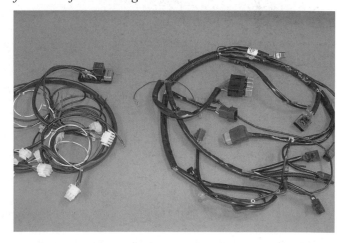

On the left, a Wiring plus kit with one 30 amp main breaker and 3 solid state 15 amp breakers, and a factory harness with the smaller 15 amp breakers.

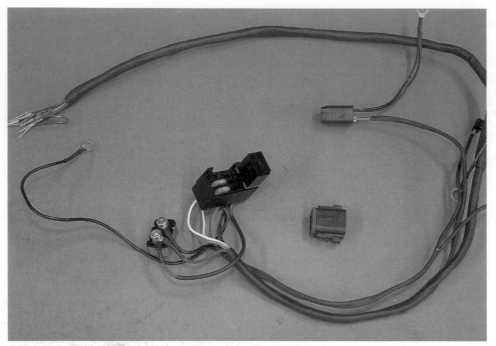

Prototype American Thunder main harness with one, 30 amp main breaker and two 15 amp fuses. All connectors are waterproof. Plugged into the module is the new-style, smaller starter relay.

chopper fork puts the wheel and caliper so far away from the handle bar master cylinder that an extra long hydraulic hose has to be made up.

Attaching the sheet metal is pretty straight forward. The front fender used here is from Harley-Davidson and utilizes linkage that keeps it close to the tire as the wheel goes over bumps. Though the Rolling Thunder frame came with the tank mounts already mounted, and all the sheet metal, it's always a good idea to check the fit of all these pieces before sending them out for paint. The tank is a one-piece design, and the rear fender is a strutless design for that smoooooth look.

CONCLUSION

As we send this book off to the printer the seat is not installed (still at the upholstery shop), but the bike is otherwise ready to fire and ride. With the springer fork and raised neck, the new machine has the look of a chopper from the early 1970s. Yet, in the good old days there were no 124 cubic inch S&S engines with electric start and automatic compression releases, or six-speed Baker right-side-drive transmissions – all available as part of a kit that makes building one of these at home a very do-able deal.

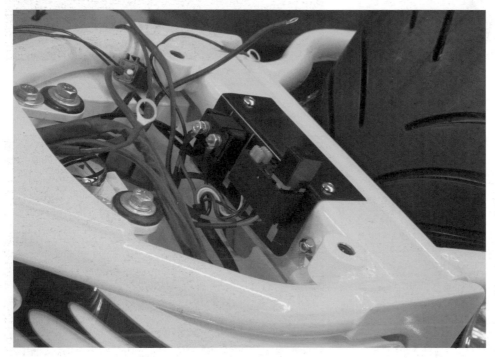

Here you see the main module bolted to the frame just behind the battery.

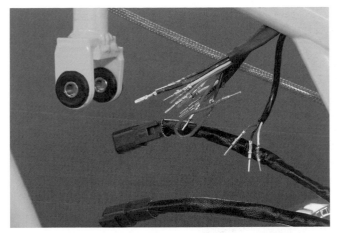

Main harness wires were run through the frame, then will be plugged into the terminal blocks. Two blocks shown are from the compression releases.

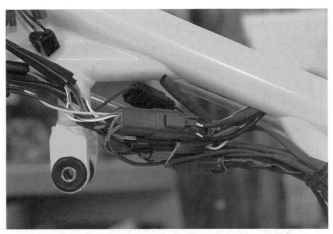

Here you can see how the main harness wires have been pushed into terminal blocks, and the blocks snapped into matching blocks.

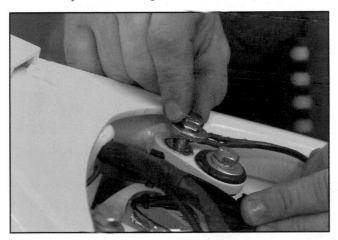

Weird electrical maladies often come from bad grounds. Be sure ground wires go to bare metal and all connections are tight.

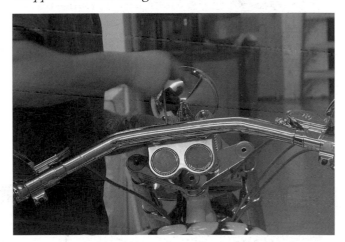

Speedo and tachometer mount to the handle bars.

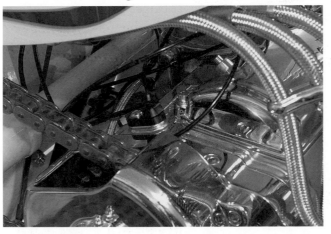

Speedometer is "driven" off the sensor (shown) in the transmission. Wire from sensor goes straight to the Dakota Digital speedo.

Basically a finished machine. All wires are plugged in and neatly routed. Battery is in place, along with the side-mount license/taillight bracket.

Chapter Eight

Paper Work

License, Title, Insure

Perhaps more important than the actual construction of the bike is the paper work, some of which you might want to do before making the actual purchase. Obtaining a legal title and insuring the bike can be challenging, exactly how challenging it is depends on where you live. Read on.

INSURANCE

When it comes to obtaining insurance for a kit bike, you can almost always buy liability coverage. The harder part is obtaining collision and theft

Whether it's a kit bike, or just a scratch built bike like this soft-tail from Perewitz, you need good paper work in order to obtain a clean title with minimal hassle.

insurance. The following insights and comments come from agents and bikers scattered across the country.

Bikers living near Brockton Massachusetts, outside Boston, often call Gil Quinn for help with insurance. Gil explained that, "each state has it's own laws. Massachusetts is unique, we have consistent insurance. No agent or company can give a quote that's better than another. At White and Quinn we make sure that when we insure a custom bike we get a certified appraisal. The bike is taken to a licensed, certified appraiser. Now when we go to the insurance company, we can give them a *stated amount*."

"For example, I've got a 1999 Road King that's fixed up. Instead of a value of sixteen thousand dollars like a standard Road King, mine is worth forty thousand dollars and I can prove it because it's been appraised. But I'm also paying insurance on a forty thousand dollar bike. The liability is the same no matter what, but the cost of theft and collision go up with the value of the bike. We also try and get all the receipts from building the bike and put them in the file. So we know what the bike is made from. Insurance companies like paper, show them paper and they're happy."

Most states don't have the certified appraisers that Gil describes. Crazy Jay, owner and manager of the Minneapolis Easyriders store has trouble with insurance on kit bikes and he suggests buyers check with their insurance agent before buying the kit.

"With no DOT sticker it's hard to get anyone to write insurance," explains Jay. "With a manufactured bike like a Big Dog or MCC, it's not a problem. Kit bikes are a big issue. The rider should check with his or her insurance agent, it could cost you a lot for insurance." Their concern, according to Jay, "is replacement parts. If you buy some one-off parts, how do they replace that part if the bike is stolen or wrecked. Their second big con-

cern is the fact that there's no started value for these bikes."

Jay, and others we spoke with, report that whether or not your agent will write more than liability on the kit bike depends in part on which companies he or she represents and also on how much other insurance you have with that agent. "Farmers will take some of these," says Jay, "but Dairyland won't take any and neither will Progressive." Obviously, if you do a large volume of other insurance business with one agent, that agent has an incentive to figure out a way to insure your project bike.

**MANUFACTURER'S
STATEMENT OF ORIGIN
TO A MOTOR CYCLE FRAME**

The undersigned CORPORATION hereby certifies that the new motorcycle frame described below, the property of said MANUFACTURER, has been transferred this 6th day of **June, 2002 on invoice 2378**

To: **American Thunder
16760 Toronto Ave. S.E.
Prior Lake, MN   USA
55372**

TYPE OF MOTORCYCLE FRAME

Style: **Softail – 250   Right Side Drive**

Shipping Weight: **91 lbs. (ninety-one)**

Year Model: **2002**

Number: **2 R T M C 0 7 2 X 2 M 0 7 2 0 8 9**

The MANUFACTURER further certifies that this was the first transfer of such new motorcycle frame in ordinary trade and commerce.

Manufacturer: **Rolling Thunder Mfg. Inc.**

Signed by: _____

              Bill Ford, Vice President

Address: **1810 Ford Boulevard
Chateauguay, Quebec
J6J 4Z2 (Canada)**

Engines and frames (and some transmissions) come with a MSO that lists the manufacturer and the serial number.

139

Deciding whether or not to ride the bike with only liability insurance depends in part on your tolerance for risk, and also on whether or not you borrowed money to buy the kit.

TITLES

When it comes to obtaining clear title to the new bike the issues are closely related to those that came up for Insurance. How difficult it will be to get a clear title for that new bike depends partly on where you live. This is another situation where it's nice to buy the kit from a local shop, where they know first hand how best to get over the official speed bumps.

"Keep all the receipts," is the mantra recited by anyone who's done this before, no matter which state they live in. The second part of that phrase is, "don't buy swap meet parts."

"If you say 'swap meet parts' at any time while you're talking to the people from the state," explains bike builder Dave Perewitz from Massachusetts, "it's like swearing in church." Jay from Easyriders is equally blunt, "'Swap meet parts' turns' on a light for the state, the light says stolen parts. In Minnesota they have two things they really watch for, one is stolen parts and the other is sales tax. Buy everything from a legitimate dealer and keep the receipts. That way you can prove that the parts are not stolen and that all the sales tax has been paid."

In Massachusetts, you have to have the *dealer's* receipts for everything, which can be hard to come by. In Minnesota, and most other states, you simply need legitimate receipts for all the parts, and an MSO (manufacturer's statement of origin) for the engine and the frame. Most companies also provide an MSO for the transmission or transmission case. Harley-Davidson provides only a receipt and most states recognize that fact.

In the past people would sometimes buy a set of engine cases, which come with a MSO, then assemble the rest of the engine with "swap meet parts." The result was a cheap engine, but most of the state authorities are so savvy now that the ploy is likely to generate nothing but trouble.

An inspection of the bike is required by many states. In Minnesota you have to take all the paper work to a local deputy registrar's office, where (assuming all the paper work is in order) they collect any additional sales tax due on the bike and issue a set of plates. At a slightly later date they will call the bike in for an inspection. Massachusetts does the inspection by the state police at a Department of Public Works garage. Dave Perewitz explains that the paper work must be turned in at the same

---

FIRST ASSIGNMENT

FOR VALUE RECEIVED, the undersigned hereby transfers this **Statement of Origin** and the motor vehicle described therein to _____
Address _____
_____
and certifies that the vehicle is new and has not been registered in this or any other state; he also warrants the title of said motor vehicle at time of delivery, subject to the liens and encumbrances, if any, as set out below.

Amt of Lien	Date	To Whom Due	Address

Date _____, at _____

_____ By: _____
Transferor (Firm Name)   (Sign Here)   (Position)

SECOND ASSIGNMENT

FOR VALUE RECEIVED, the undersigned hereby transfers this **Statement of Origin** and the motor vehicle described therein to _____
Address _____
_____
and certifies that the vehicle is new and has not been registered in this or any other state; he also warrants the title of said motor vehicle at time of delivery, subject to the liens and encumbrances, if any, as set out below.

Amt of Lien	Date	To Whom Due	Address

Date _____, at _____

_____ By: _____
Transferor (Firm Name)   (Sign Here)   (Position)

THIRD ASSIGNMENT

FOR VALUE RECEIVED, the undersigned hereby transfers this **Statement of Origin** and the motor vehicle described therein to _____
Address _____
_____
and certifies that the vehicle is new and has not been registered in this or any other state; he also warrants the title of said motor vehicle at time of delivery, subject to the liens and encumbrances, if any, as set out below.

Amt of Lien	Date	To Whom Due	Address

Date _____, at _____

_____ By: _____
Transferor (Firm Name)   (Sign Here)   (Position)

The back side records the transfer of ownership from the manufacturer to the buyer, and any additional transfers from buyer to buyer.

time, and that the bike must be equipped with all the standard items spelled out by law.

Not all titles are created equal. Many states classify kit bikes and any motorcycles assembled from parts as a reconstructed vehicle, with a special title, much like a car that's been rebuilt from a wreck. Cory Ness reports that California classifies bikes built in their shop as "special construction." Minnesota recently changed the law, following plenty of lobbying by the MMRA (Minnesota Motorcycle Riders Association), so that now bikes assembled from parts are titled as a standard motorcycle, though it might be called a RevTech, Daytec or Biker's Choice depending on who manufactured the frame.

Just a few more pointers. The state has been know to loose the paper work you so carefully saved. So make at least one copy of all the receipts and relevant paper work. A photo file might not be a bad idea either.

MONEY

You can borrow money against a Harley-Davidson, and often against a recognized brand like a Big Dog, because the bikes have established values the loan officer can look up in a price book. Kit bikes have no such established value, so you probably can't get a banker to loan you money on the machine – especially when it exists only as a large pile of parts.

Jay suggests an old fashioned alternative. "We've sold some of these at the store and the buyers need to have cash."

Another option is to borrow money against the house or another asset like a motorcycle or even a car that you own free and clear. Option number three would be to buy everything on the credit card and then try to get a regular loan once the bike is assembled and you can show the loan officer that it is a real, running motorcycle. Obviously the issue of financing will be related to insurance. If the bike *is* financed, the company holding the paper on the machine will want it insured for theft and collision.

A mix of methods might be best for most would-be-builders. Save up as much cash as possible and supplement that with a modest amount of credit card debt, or a personal loan from the credit union. If you don't have a twenty thousand dollar note against the bike it's easier to accept the idea of riding it around with nothing but liability insurance - and a big hairy lock.

Whether or not you need turn signals for the state inspection depends on the state. Rob Roehl registered this little chopper based on a Redneck frame in Minnesota without any hassles. Be sure the state can read the VIN numbers on the neck.

Wolfgang Books On The Web

http://www.wolfgangpublications.com

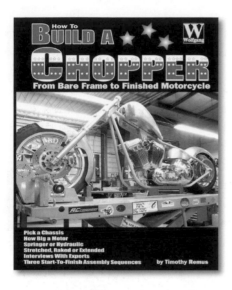

HOW TO BUILD A CHOPPER

Choppers are back! Learn from the best how to build yours.
12 chapters cover:
- Use of Evo, TC, Shovel, Pan or Knucklehead engines
- Frame and running gear choices
- Design decisions - short and stubby or long and radical?
- Four, five or six-speed trannies
- Over 300 photos-over 50% color

Designed to help you build your own chopper, this book covers History, Frames, Chassis Components, Wheels and Tires, Engine Options, Drivetrains, Wiring, Sheet Metal and Hardware. Included are assembly sequences from the Arlen Ness, Donnie Smith and American Thunder shops. Your best first step! Order today.

Twelve Chapters   144 Pages $24.95

BUILD THE ULTIMATE V-TWIN CHASSIS

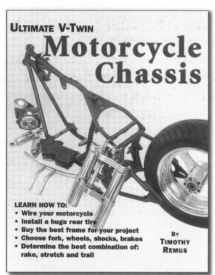

Ten chapters with 250+ photos.
- Frame buyers guide
- Which fork to buy
- Installing the driveline
- Sheet metal choices
- Powder coat or paint
- Mount a super wide rear tire
- How to pick the best brakes
- Understand motorcycle wiring

The foundation of any custom or scratch-built motorcycle is the frame. The look, ride and handling are all determined by the chassis. This book is part Buyer's Guide and part Assembly Manual. Shop Tours of Arlen Ness and M-C Specialties. Newly revised.

Ten Chapters   144 Pages $19.95

AMERICAN V-TWIN ENGINE

Everything you need to build or buy the right V-twin motor for your dream ride. Informative text illustrated with more than 300 photos.

- TC History
- TC Development
- TC 88-B
- TC Troubles
- TC Hop Up
- TC Cam & Big-Bore install
- Evo Planning
- Evo Carbs

- Evo Cams
- Evo Head & Porting
- Evo Combinations
- Evo Big Block Engines
- Evo Cam Install & Engine Assembly
 A large Sources section

Fourteen Chapters   160 Pages $21.95

More Great Books From Wolfgang Publications!

http://www.wolfgangpublications.com

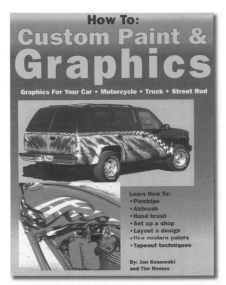

HOW TO: CUSTOM PAINT & GRAPHICS

Over 250 photos, 50% in color
7 chapters include:
- Shop tools and equipment
- Paint and materials
- Letter & pinstripe by hand
- Design and tapeouts
- Airbrushing
- Hands-on, Flames and signs
- Hands-on, Graphics

A joint effort of the master of custom painting, Jon Kosmoski and Tim Remus, this is the book for anyone who wants to try their hand at dressing up their street rod, truck or motorcycle with lettering, flames or exotic graphics. A great companion to Kustom Painting Secrets (below).

Seven Chapters   144 Pages $24.95

KUSTOM PAINTING SECRETS

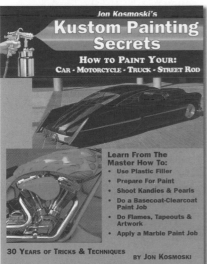

250 photos with color section
7 chapters include:
- History of House of Kolor
- How to Set up a shop
- Color painting sequences
- Prepare for paint
- Final paint application
- Hands-on, basic paint jobs
- Hands-on, beyond basic paint

- Hands-on, custom painting
More from the master! From the basics to advanced custom painting tricks, Jon Kosmoski shares his 30 years of experience in this book. Photos by publisher Tim Remus bring Jon's text to life. A must for ayone interested in the art of custom painting.

Seven Chapters   128 Pages $19.95

ULTIMATE SHEET METAL FABRICATION

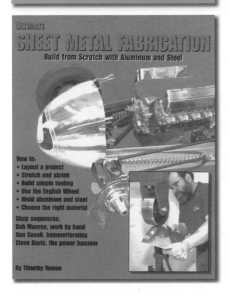

Over 350 photos
11 chapters include:
- Layout a project
- Pick the right material
- Shrinkers & stretchers
- English wheel
- Make & use simple tooling
- Weld aluminum or steel
- Use hand and power tools

In an age when most products are made by the thousands, many yearn for the one-of-kind metal creation. Whether you're building or restoring a car, motorcycle, airplane or (you get the idea), you'll find the information you need to custom build your own parts from steel or aluminum.

Eleven Chapters   144 Pages $19.95

Sources

Air Lift
Handy Industries,
LLC
Marshall town IA
800 437 0190
641 752 1205

American Thunder
16760 Toronto Avenue
Prior Lake, MN 55372
952 226 1180

Accurate Engineering
128 Southgate Road
Dolhan, AL 36301
334 702 1993

Arlen Ness Inc.
16520 E 14th St.
San Leandro, CA 94578
510 276 3395

Baker Transmissions
9804 E Saginaw
Haslett, MI 48840
517 339 3835

Best Coat Inc
Powder Coating
1557 101st Av N.E.
Blaine, MN 55449
763 785 7086

Biker's Choice
www.bikerschoice.com

Chimaera
Small Stainless clamps
16 Higgins Dr
Milford, CT 06460

Chrome Specialties Inc.
4200 Diplomacy Road
Fort Worth, TX 76155
800 277 8685 to find a dealer.
www.chromespecialties.com

Custom Chrome
800 359 5700
www.customchrome.com

Cyril Huze Customs
3601 N. Dixie Hwy #11
Boca Raton, FL 33431
561 347 1616
www.cyrilhuze.com

Delano Harley-Davidson
4354 US Hwy 12 SE
Delano, MN 55328
763 479-2530

Donnie Smith Custom Cycles
10594 Raddison Road NE
Blaine, MN 55449
612 786 6002

Easyriders MPLS
904 19th Ave. So.
MPLS MN 55404
Phone: 612 340 0400

Knucklehead Power USA
5715 Pinkney Avenue
Sarasota, FL 34233
941 921 4762

Johnson, Kendall
Killer Klown wheels and killer V-twins
8720 Dennis Road
Germanton, NC 27019
336 595 9339

Jim's Manufacturing
531 Dawson Drive Unit F
Camarillo, CA 93012
805 482 6913

Neve, Kyle
(Painter of Goliath)
Phone: 336 983 7796

Performance Machine
6892 Marlin Circle
LaPalma, CA 90623
714 523 3000

Perewitz, Dave
Cycle Fabrications
909 North Main St.
Brockton, MA 02401
508 586-2511

Rivera Engineering
12532 Lambert Road
Whittier, CA 90606
562 907 2600

Rolling Thunder
1810 Ford Boulevard
Chateauguay, QC J6J 4Z2 CAN
450 699 7045
www.rollingthunderframes.com

TP Engineering
5 Frances J. Clarke Circle
Bethel, CT 06801
203 744 4960

S&S Cycle
Box 215 - RT 2, County G
Viola, WI 54664
608 627 1497

White and Quinn Insurance
Agency
2331 Mass Ave.
Cambridge, MA 02140
617 876 2512

Zipper's Cycle Inc.
6655A Amberton Drive
Elkridge, MD 21075
410 579 2100